the book of

Amos

Henry Vander Kam

Reformed Fellowship, Inc.
3363 Hickory Ridge Ct. SW
Grandville, MI 49418

©2007 Reformed Fellowship, Inc.
Printed in the United States of America.
All rights reserved

For information:
Reformed Fellowship, Inc.
3363 Hickory Ridge Ct. SW
Grandville, MI 49418
Phone: 616.532.8510
Web: reformedfellowship.net
Email: sales@reformedfellowship.net

Book design by Jeff Steenholdt

ISBN 0-9793677-1-9

Contents

Outline of Lessons

Introduction

Amos was one of the earliest prophets whose writings have been incorporated in the canon of Scripture. This seems strange because this book is very up-to-date. When one studies the book of Amos he wonders whether this book was not written especially for a time such as this.

Nothing is known of the writer of this book save that which we find in the book itself. There is no reference to him in any of the historical books of the Old Testament. Amos introduces himself to the readers of his book in the first verse of the first chapter and refers to his vocation and calling in chapter 7:14-15. Only three verses are used to tell us who he is, where he lived, when he prophesied, how he made his living, and why he became a prophet. But, as is characteristic of Amos, he can say much in few words.

Amos lived in Tekoa, about twelve miles south of Jerusalem. It is situated in rugged, hilly country. Here he was a herdsman and a dresser of sycamore trees. It is difficult to tell with certainty from the word used whether he was the owner of a flock or whether he was a shepherd in the employ of others. Did he raise sycamore trees or was its fruit his food? Again, it is difficult to state the matter with any degree of certainty. He seems to have been neither rich nor poor, but was able to leave his work for some time to prophesy.

Amos did not come from one of "the schools of the prophets." He was not a professional. He was taken from his daily work and was told to bring a very specific message to Israel. Yet, though he did not receive instruction at any

1

school for his prophetic task, the whole book bears testimony to the fact that he was a talented man. Many of his statements may not sound very polished but there is also a certain poetic eloquence. His style is vivid. He uses illustrations from his former employment very effectively. His style suits his message admirably.

Amos prophesied during the time when Uzziah was king of Judah and Jeroboam II was king of Israel. This places the time of his ministry in approximately the middle of the eighth century before the coming of Christ. He prophesied two years before the earthquake. Many earthquakes have shaken the land of Palestine but this was the most memorable one. The prophet Zechariah makes reference to this same earthquake (Zech. 14:5).

Although Amos was from Judah he was called to prophesy in and against Israel, the northern kingdom. Once before, in the days of Jeroboam I, a man of God had been sent from Judah to bring the word of God against Israel. When Amos speaks he is on foreign soil. Yet, he is well acquainted with conditions in Samaria, having, no doubt, often been to the markets there.

Amos is called for a very specific task. God places his own words in the mouth of the prophets. Amos will speak only the words which he "saw," and the visions which he saw. "Jehovah will roar from Zion." Amos will not come to speak peace to the northern kingdom. His prophecies are full of judgment. Jehovah's voice will thunder. The pastures of the shepherds and the top of Carmel will be scorched! No living thing will be able to endure the wrath of God. The voice of Jehovah will be heard from Jerusalem. Jeroboam I had introduced false worship in are the northern kingdom. Baal was served during the days of Ahab. Elijah warred against this Baal worship and was successful in uprooting it to a large degree. At the present time the people of Israel serve "Jehovah." Let them realize

that Jehovah's house is in Judah and that he dwells
in Jerusalem!

Why is Amos sent with such a message of judgment
against Israel? The whole book of Amos gives an answer to
this question. The conditions in the land of Israel were such
that one marvels that the earthquake of which he spoke did
not come earlier.

There was more prosperity in both Israel and Judah than
at any time since the reign of Solomon. Jeroboam II had
extended the borders of Israel farther than ever before.
He had been successful in war. No nation threatened the
peace of Israel. Commerce and industry flourished. Time
and again Amos refers to the wealth of the people of Israel.
Wealth gave them social position. It brought ease. They
could afford "a good life." This led to all manner of evils.

But, religion was not forgotten! In fact, the people were
very religious. The requirements of the law were held in
honor. They cannot understand why Amos preaches coming
judgment. God has blest them as never before. Is this not an
indication of Divine favor? Let this man talk; but they will
not listen. His message is even irritating. Let him go back
where he came from (Amos 7:12-13).

Jehovah roars from Zion. The people think they are
serving Jehovah, but it is not the God of their fathers.
They have made a god in their own image! Amos will tell
them who God is and what he requires. Their religion is
false. They worship as they see fit. The fact, that religion is
practiced does not necessarily mean that it will meet with
the favor of God. It must be true religion. True religion is
basic to morality. The people of Israel know no morality.
The thirst for wealth determines their business practices.
Immoral deeds are committed which are not even found
among the heathen. This is indicative of the shallowness of
their religion.

Amos first spoke these prophecies in Israel. Later they

were written in the book which is now before us. Thus these prophecies were preserved for the church of all ages. Amos pictures the times vividly. He also reveals the God who is not mocked. The times, as Amos describes them, remind us of our own time. This book could have been written yesterday! Although his message is one of judgment against the evils of his day, mercy is not forgotten. The remnant shall be saved. The tabernacle of David which has fallen shall be raised up again. So Amos speaks to us today.

Questions for Discussion

1. Why do you think it is very important for the understanding of a Bible book to know who the author is, where he lived, etc.?
2. Why does the talent of the author of a Bible book influence his style of writing, seeing the Spirit of God has inspired all authors?
3. Amos did not attend the schools of the prophets but God called him directly. Is such a thing still possible today?
4. Is prosperity always a sign of Divine favor?
5. Does our religion today sufficiently govern our daily lives?
6. Do you think there is enough preaching in our circles on such themes as are treated in the book of Amos? If not, how would you explain this lack?

The Judgments on the Nations – I

Amos 1:3-8

Amos was sent to speak against the land of Israel, and now... he speaks against the surrounding nations! For a moment the people were startled. His opening words were placed in the framework of judgment; but this is better! Let him condemn the nations that know not God!

However, notice the order which the prophet follows. There is a definite pattern. Be sure to consult a map. Amos begins with the nations rather far distant from Samaria. Slowly the circle becomes smaller, and...the last one is Israel. Let the people not rejoice too quickly.

The very fact that the prophet speaks first of the judgment which is to fall on the nations shows the people that the jurisdiction of their God is not restricted. He is God of all the earth. He is the Almighty. The heathen nations are his concern too. The iniquity of the heathen will not go unpunished.

The formula which Amos uses to introduce the prophecy of judgment on the nations is the same for each one. "For three transgressions... yea, for four, I will not turn away the punishment thereof." One transgression would make them worthy of death. "Three transgressions" denotes a full measure of iniquity; and four is an overflowing measure. God has waited long enough. He is slow to anger, patient and longsuffering. However, when there is an overflowing measure of iniquity, he will wait no longer.

It is settled. "I will not turn away the punishment thereof."
The first judgment is pronounced against Syria. No wonder!
How brutal and inhuman the Syrians were! God sometimes
uses the heathen nations to chastise his people, but let them
beware that they go no farther than he permits. The Syrians
invaded Gilead in the past. This was that part of the land of
Israel that lay east of the Jordan River. God had permitted
the Syrians to invade this part of the country, but they
slaughtered the people cruelly. They should have
remembered the words, "Gilead is mine" (Psalm 60:7).
Because of their wicked deeds, God will send fire on the
dynasty of Syria. The royal house shall be destroyed. Hazael
had been anointed king over Syria by the prophet Elisha.
After the anointing the old prophet wept when he was given
to see prophetically the cruelty which Hazael would show
to Israel. The judgment is now sure. Damascus will be
invaded. The inhabitants of two unknown places are
named. These will be destroyed. Syria will go into captivity
to the place from whence they had come (Amos 9:7).
Syria had been a great power, but its days are numbered.
They came from Kir — they will go back to Kir. There has
been no progress at all for this heathen power. Heathendom
has no future.

The second judgment is pronounced against Philistia.
This was one of the oldest enemies of Israel. David had
fought many of his battles against this war-like people.
Will Philistia finally receive its just reward? Israel hopes so.
Thus Amos is speaking words which they love to hear.
Let the surrounding nations be judged so that Israel may
prosper! Syria was to the northeast, Philistia to the
southwest. Israel does not yet realize that God's judgments
are closing in and will also strike the northern kingdom.

Philistia's measure of iniquity is also overflowing. Many
evils had been committed against God's people by the
Philistines but Amos mentions only one. God had used also

the Philistines to chastise Israel in the past. When Israel
sinned God allowed the Philistines to come into the land
and plunder it. But Philistia was not satisfied with this role.
They did not want to chastise, they wanted to destroy.
Therefore God will not turn away their punishment.

The specific sin of Philistia to which the prophet refers is
the sin of leading people into captivity. This was a rather
common practice in Old Testament times. Later both Judah
and Israel were led into captivity. Philistia, however, did
more. They carried away captive "the whole people."
This does not mean that all the people of the nation were
carried captive, but that whole towns or districts were led
captive. Didn't other nations do the same thing? Yes, but
Philistia did more. They were not satisfied with leading
conquered people captive to their own land; they delivered
them up to Edom. *They traded in people!* They made slaves
of the conquered people and sold them to the Edomites.
God's people were placed on the slave block in the cities of
the Philistines. Jehovah will not allow this to go
unpunished. Slavery was forbidden in Israel. Although his
people have sinned he still watches over them. He will not
allow families to be torn apart. He has led them out of
slavery and woe to the nation which enslaves them again!

Philistia's punishment will be similar to the punishment to
come upon the land of Syria. He will send a fire on the wall
of Gaza and its palaces will be destroyed. That fire need not
be the kind of fire which fell from heaven to destroy Sodom
and Gomorrah. It may refer to the fire of war or other
devastation. The other principal cities of the Philistines will
likewise be punished. The inhabitants of Ashdod will be cut
off. The rulers of Ashkelon will be cut off. God will turn his
hand against Ekron. Uzziah had in recent years destroyed
the city of Gath (II Chron. 26:6). All the major cities will be
laid waste. Even the remnant of the Philistines will perish.
The destruction of this ancient enemy of Israel will be

complete. Never again will Israel have to fear this people.

These are not the words of a mere man; God has spoken them. Amos is only giving utterance to the words or visions of "the Lord Jehovah" which he "saw." That is the name of God which Amos uses again and again. This is the God who rules all things and all peoples. His word will come true. When God gives his promise, the thing promised is already real; when he pronounces judgment the judgment is already real. "Let the nations know themselves to be but men" (Psalm 9:20).

Questions for Discussion

1. We bring the Gospel to the heathen with the intension of bringing them to salvation; should we also warn them of God's judgments on the nations?
2. Why should we be much concerned about the evils committed by the heathen?
3. Why is it that the heathen are said to have no "excuse?" (Rom. 1:20)
4. Does God still use the heathen to chastise His people?
5. What comfort is it to you that God rules the world as well as the church?

The Judgments on the Nations – II

Amos 1:9-12

The third nation condemned for its wickedness by the prophet Amos is Tyre. This nation was quite far to the northwest from the land of Israel.

The reason for the condemnation of Tyre seems to be virtually the same as that of Philistia. Both dealt in the slave trade. Tyre's sin is not as grievous as Philistia's because nothing is said concerning the *capture* of slaves, but only their *sale* of slaves to Edom. The slave market was not confined to one nation. Various nations made themselves guilty of this practice.

However, it is not only the slave trade which has occasioned the prophet's condemnation of Tyre. That nation is also guilty of not remembering the brotherly covenant. This does not mean that Israel had made a covenant with Tyre. God's people were constantly warned not to enter into covenants or alliances with the heathen. Had such a covenant of brotherliness been broken, the prophet would have rejoiced.

The covenant to which reference is made is no doubt the covenant made between Solomon and Hiram the king of Tyre (I Kings 5). This was a covenant of trade. Hiram calls Solomon "my brother" (I Kings 9:13). This was a brotherly covenant. The best relations had existed also between David and Hiram. This is now the sin of Tyre that they have not remembered this brotherly covenant. Agreements are for gotten. They are become meaningless. This overturns the good-will relationship among nations. Confidence is destroyed. If such covenants are conveniently forgotten, there will be no honor among nations.

God is interested in the pacts between nations. He is very much concerned about the business dealings among men. Tyre is quite a distance from Samaria, but Jehovah's roar is now heard distinctly even in Israel. The evils mentioned before were abominations also in the eyes of the Israelites. But God will destroy even a nation which does not honor business commitments. That touches Israel. Israel's commerce and industry are flourishing. Is it not enough that Israel brings sacrifices, pays its tithes, and sings David's Psalms? Will God also look sharply at their business ethics? He will and still does. Tyre will be destroyed because it remembered not the brotherly covenant. Nations and individuals are destroyed not only because of atheism or immorality, but also because of corruption in business! The God of Amos, the God of the Bible, the Father of our Lord Jesus Christ, is a God who requires justice, also in the economic world.

The next nation to which the prophet turns his attention is Edom. This land was situated southeast of Israel. The Edomites are the descendants of Esau. There was a close historical tie to Edom. Esau and Jacob were brothers — twin brothers. Israel is the people of promise — Esau is condemned. Although Israel was more closely related to Edom than to the previously mentioned nations, the enmity was greater.

There is really no specific sin mentioned for which Edom will be destroyed. It is rather an *attitude*. There had been enmity from the beginning. Jacob and Esau were twins — but there all similarity ceased. They did not look alike. They didn't have the same interests. Most important of all, one was a believer and the other an unbeliever. Jacob fled from

home because he feared Esau. He was afraid when he met
Esau on his return at the Jabbok. Edom refused to give
Israel permission to travel through its land when Israel was
approaching Canaan. That pursuit with the sword went on
through the ages.

Edom never showed pity. Esau was a rough and calloused
individual and his descendants had the same trait. There
was no feeling for their blood-relationship to Israel. Those
who stand in the closest relationship toward each other
often show the least pity.

Edom's anger "tears," rages, perpetually and he kept his
wrath forever. There is no forgiving spirit. Jacob had not
always dealt in a brotherly manner with Esau. He had much
to confess. But is there no forgiving spirit even among
brethren? Not with Esau. His anger "tears" (ch. 1:11) and
he keeps his wrath. He does not only *fall* into sin, he *lives*
in sin. This anger and wrath produces the sword wherewith
he pursues his brother. It is the root of murder!

The attitude displayed by Edom toward Israel has
seemingly stirred the emotions of the prophet. Philistia and
Tyre were guilty of delivering slaves to *Edom*. Edom had
made itself guilty of slave traffic. However, the prophet does
not even mention this evil when he speaks of Edom directly.
Although that slave traffic will not go unpunished, the
attitude of hatred which Edom had shown to Israel is even
more grievous. It is the attitude which is capable of
committing virtually every sin. There was no penitence.
Esau was grieved when he did not receive the blessing of his
father (Heb. 12:17), but it was not genuine penitence. His
descendants had that same impenitent spirit. God's wrath is
kindled against hatred of brethren. His wrath is kindled
against the unforgiving spirit. Impenitence removes the
possibility of salvation!

Because of the attitude of Edom the fires will rage
there too. The punishment of this *attitude* of hatred is the

same as the punishment of the overt evils committed by the other nations named earlier.

The whole prophecy is directed toward Israel. Let them be warned! God does not only punish corrupt business practices in Tyre and ungodly attitudes in Edom; he punishes such things wherever they are found. These things are written for the benefit of the church of all ages. God's anger burns against these evils. He will roar from Zion and utter his voice from Jerusalem. That roar, that warning, must be sounded by the church. There God dwells. The voice of the church, the voice of the living God must be raised against the evils of our day... or we shall likewise perish.

Questions for Discussion

1. Can a Christian be in business today? Are there difficulties, and, if so, what are these difficulties?
2. Is fair business dealing regarded as important as true confession? Is it as important?
3. Is it sin for nations to break treaties?
4. Is it always a sin for an individual not to meet his financial commitments?
5. Should the church speak out more freely against social evils? If she does, will this make her gospel a "social gospel"?
6. How long may we be angry with a brother?
7. Do we ever truly forgive? Is it possible to forgive and forget?

The Judgments on the Nations – III

Amos 1:13-2:3

Again the prophet raises his voice to speak judgment to the nations. Now it is coming much closer to Israel. Judgment is closing in. When Amos completes the list of nations ripe for judgment, Israel will see the whole surrounding world lie in ruin. At present he is still speaking against the enemies of Israel. They will be destroyed. Israel listens enraptured to this prophet.

The nations to whom the prophet now directs his attention were also related to Israel. Ammon and Moab were the descendants of Lot. These were not as closely related to Israel as Edom was, but nevertheless, they were related.

Ammon was the son of Lot's youngest daughter. The sordid history of the birth of Ammon and Moab is recorded in Gen. 19. Lot was their father although he should have been their grandfather. Lot had lived near and in Sodom too long. Lot was a righteous man (II Peter 2:7) but his family was brought up in Sodom. The sin of Sodom had its effect on his daughters. These girls had no moral principles. How can the children born of such mothers ever amount to anything? The sins of Sodom continue in the descendants of Lot. He remained righteous; his children become the victims of their early surroundings.

What was the sin of Ammon? It was the sin of sadistic cruelty. Sodom had been destroyed but all the effects of its sin have not been wiped out. "They have ripped up the women with child of Gilead." How low can man fall? How the divine image is obscured when man does such beastly things! Other nations have come and destroyed all the living. Others have come and carried the people away captive. Ammon goes a step farther. They not only slay the living, but destroy even the unborn generations. Civilized man has become savage. This evil was committed against God's people in Gilead.

Was it only to satisfy their own lust that they committed this awful sin? Amos is more specific. They did these savage things for one purpose: that they may enlarge their borders. The land which Gilead occupies cannot be occupied by Ammon. Therefore, destroy Gilead so that our borders may be enlarged! Destroy the future generations so that our occupancy may never be jeopardized! So Ammon judges — but God judges differently.

The God of Amos utters his voice against Ammon's cruelty. He also visits the sin of destroying the unborn. Children are a blessing of Jehovah. Gilead's children belonged to him. He will avenge. Let Israel listen closely. Let the church of our day also lay this to heart.

Ammon will be destroyed. Fire shall be kindled in the land of Ammon which will destroy its palaces. Besides the fire there will be battle and tempest and whirlwind. Here is a description of a day of judgment. His fire, the enemy's sword, and the powers of nature will be loosed against the land of Ammon for the sins they have committed.

Now the prophet turns his eyes to Moab. Moab and Ammon are, of course, closely related. How are they related? When sin desecrates the ordinances of God that relationship becomes very involved. Moab and Ammon are cousins; but they are also brothers. Both were the products of sin.

Ammon's sin is easily traceable to the land where his mother had lived so long. Moab committed sin of a different nature. The previous nations had all made themselves guilty by committing their sins against the people of God. Moab sins against Edom. That God watches over his own is something we expect. The Bible is full of it. But he also watches over those who are not his people.

What was Moab's chief sin? "He burned the bones of the king of Edom into lime." Was that so bad? Look what Edom had done to Israel! Didn't Edom deserve to be treated the way Moab treated him? Many would conclude that the hatred of Edom for Israel had removed all of Edom's rights and that no disgrace would be enough for him. So man judges — but God judges differently.

Moab had cremated the body of the king of Edom. Whether he had fallen in battle or whether his grave had been dishonored, we do not know. Is cremation wrong? Is it not the best way of disposing of the body? Is it not better for the health of the living? Will it not save a great amount of land which is so sorely needed by the teeming millions on this earth? Such questioning satisfies man's conscience — but God judges differently.

Edom was not God's people. Nay, the father of this people — Esau — I hated, says the Lord. Yet, God protects the rights of Edom. Although Edom is not his child, he bears the divine image. That image of God may not be disgraced by others. Burial is honorable according to Scripture. A decent burial was highly esteemed. If a king was extremely wicked he would not be buried with his fathers. This was the final humiliation. Cremation was an abomination in the sight of God. Isaiah 33:12 refers to the same thing. The greatest evil to come upon the altar erected by Jeroboam I was the burning of men's bones upon it (I Kings 13:2). Cremation is an attempt to destroy, to annihilate. God's honor is at stake. His image is to be treated honorably.

The destruction of Moab will also be complete. The fire

will rage there too. However, an additional element is introduced. "Moab shall die with tumult, with shouting, and with the sound of the trumpet." This sounds more like feasting. Jeremiah had called the Moabites "the tumultuous ones" (Jer. 48:45). They lived noisily and boisterously. So shall they also die. The funeral of Moab will be like the life he has lived. Funeral orations do not change the judgment.

Questions for Discussion

1. Why does the Bible give us the story of the sins of Lot and others? How does this differ from the "realism" of our day?
2. If Lot maintained his righteousness in Sodom, why didn't this influence his daughters as much as the sin of Sodom?
3. Is Malthusianism, i.e., the theory of restricting the growth of population, a great evil today?
4. When one seeks to increase or enlarge his own borders is this usually at the expense of the Kingdom of God?
5. Why must we be as sensitive to the evils committed against the heathen as to those committed against God's people?
6. Why is cremation wrong?
7. Is a eulogy at a funeral wrong?

Lesson 5

The Judgment on Judah and Israel

Amos 2:4-8

The judgment is coming closer. It began in far-off Damascus.
It has circled about Israel (consult a map). The whole
surrounding heathen world is on fire. The thunder-claps
are becoming louder. Now it strikes Judah! God's covenant
people! Jerusalem, where his name would dwell forever!
Israel has listened with increasing interest to this —
prophet, but this particular prophecy disturbs them.
However, the storm is still some distance away and there is
no immediate danger. Besides, Judah has been no friend of
Israel for many years even though they are closely related.
And Judah always considered herself a little "better" than
Israel. Was not the temple in Jerusalem? Were his kings not
of the line of David to whom the promises had been given?
Now the fires of God are coming to devour the palaces of
Jerusalem. Surely, this will slay her pride.

Again the same formula is used. "For three transgressions
of Judah, yea, for four, I will not turn away the punishment
thereof" (See Lesson 2-P. 3). yet, the transgressions are not
so clearly spelled out. The prophet says that they have
rejected the law of God; they have not kept his statutes.
In other words, it is not so much what they have *done* as
what they have *not done*. The terrible deeds of the heathen
which were described before are certainly worthy of
God's judgment. That is immediately evident. But Judah is
not accused of these sins. Her sin is a sin of omission. We

usually deal much more kindly with such sin than with the
actual sinful deeds. God doesn't. In his sight the sin of
omission is as evil as the sin of commission. God gave his
people his law. Therein he spoke to them. Their sin is that
they "just let him talk" and pay no attention. They have
ignored him. There is no greater evil than that.

The prophet also refers to their idolatry. Those are "their
lies" which "have caused them to err, after which their
fathers did walk." Judah was God's chosen people. He only
was their God. Judah was not satisfied with this
relationship. They transgressed the very first commandment.
Other gods were imported. Their fathers had done the same
thing. But how their fathers paid for this evil! Though
history was able to teach them such a lesson, they did not
listen but walked the same path their fathers walked. The
measure of their iniquity is now full. God will send a fire on
Judah which will devour the palaces of Jerusalem.

Now the lightning strikes! "For three transgressions of
Israel, yea, for four, I will not turn away the punishment
thereof." They should have expected it. The prophet came
to Israel to prophesy against *Israel*. He had spoken of the
judgments of God on all the surrounding nations. It was
like a tightening noose. The day of wrath has come.

How the prophet goes into detail! Although the other
nations had committed many sins so that the measure of
their iniquity was full, the prophet mentioned only one sin.
Now he names the various evils committed in Israel. The sin
of Israel is that it has trodden the poor under foot. There is
no mercy. They have sold the righteous for silver and the
needy for a pair of shoes. Did they sell slaves so cheap?
No, the idea is that they made slaves of those who owed
but a very small sum. In Israel one could sell himself to his
creditor if his debts became too great. Such a one could also
demand the services of the one who owed him money.
But, even though one owes very little, the amount necessary

for a pair of shoes, as Amos says, he is sold. This goes directly contrary to the whole intent of the law.

They pant after the dust of the earth on the head of the poor. They do not rest until they have brought sorrow to the poor, of which dust on the head is a symbol. The meek are mistreated. There is no justice. The rich become richer at the expense of the poor. God had given his laws to Israel to prevent poverty. He is the defender of the widow, the orphan, the stranger, and the poor. Israel has set the law aside and seeks only its own profit.

A man and his father go unto the same maiden. The maiden referred to is the one who works in the home of the rich. She is a servant, a maid. Here again we find the oppression of the poor. But the evil-doers go a step farther. Immorality accompanies their greed. Oh, she is only a servant! She belongs to the class who have no rights. Her employer and his son commit immoral acts with her. It is repulsive in every way and goes directly contrary to that which God commanded Israel from the beginning. What can this maid do? She is helpless and becomes the victim of the rich.

Concerning the other nations the prophet mentioned only one sin even though they had committed three, and even four transgressions. Now he mentions all four. These same people, these rich, have taken the clothes of the poor in pledge, as surety. The law stated that these clothes taken in pledge had to be returned before nightfall. That is forgotten. Notice, they now lie down on these clothes *beside their altars*. They are worshipping! This is the practice of their religion. Some of their debtors were not able to pay in money — so they paid their debts in wine, the product of their vineyards. The rich now drink this wine (on feast days) in the house of their God. What hypocrisy! They are still religious as to form, but the power has been denied. God will judge this people as well as the heathen who have made themselves guilty of monstrous sins.

The judgments on the surrounding nations were but an introduction to the real intent of this prophecy. Against this background the sins of Israel are indeed black. What a masterful approach!

The sins of Israel are common even today. Neither are they recognized so readily. The sins of heathendom are immediately evident, but Israel sins in such a "civilized" manner. The people that worship may hide sins as grievous as those of the atheist! Israel was complacent but Amos has come to disturb that complacency.

Questions for Discussion

1. Why did the Israelites enjoy the "sermon" of Amos until now?
2. Prove from Scripture that the sins of omission are as grievous as the sins of commission in the sight of God. Do we evaluate them differently, and if so, why?
3. Which idols does modern man serve?
4. Why are the needy also called the righteous?
5. Are the poor mistreated in our circles today? If so, how? Who are the poor? Discuss.
6. What are some of the real dangers in our prosperity today?
7. How can it be recognized that one's religion is genuine?

Lesson 6

The Reason for Israel's Punishment

Amos 2:9-16

The previous verses have given reason enough why the judgment should fall on Israel as well as on the surrounding nations. In the verses 6 through 8 a summary is given of the sins committed in Israel. Amos is sent to prophesy against Israel and, consequently, the remainder of the book will go into detail concerning the evils of which Israel is guilty.

In this passage (Amos 2:9-16) we hear God's complaint against his people. He relates what he has done for them and what their reaction has been. Because of this reaction he will send his punishments upon the land.

If Israel will only look back into its own history it will see what God has done for this people in the past. That history should humble them. That history ought to drive them into his arms. They have been favored as no other nation.

He brought them into the land where they now dwell. That land was hostile. Before they arrived that land was peopled by giants. In comparison to the inhabitants of Canaan they looked like grasshoppers. They would never have been able to conquer this people themselves. God destroyed the Amorite before them! The first strong-hold, Jericho, fell without battle. By the term *Amorite* the prophet means all the former inhabitants.

If they will look back a little bit further into their own history, they will see that God delivered them from Egyptian slavery and carried them through the wilderness. He destroyed and plundered Egypt for their sakes. Those forty long years in the wilderness were the result of their own sin, but God used them for their welfare. He fed them during all those years. He prepared them for the conquest of Palestine. No, one does not look back with pleasure on those forty years in the wilderness, but what a marvel of divine grace that even the wrath of man shall praise him!

Although Israel was to receive the land of Canaan as its inheritance, it was not to walk in the ways of Canaan's former inhabitants. Therefore God raised up prophets and Nazirites. The prophets would warn the people and teach them the fear of God. The Nazirites were to show the people by their example that they were the peculiar people of God. What did Israel do? They gave wine to the Nazirites. These Nazirites, as Samson and Samuel, had taken a vow not to drink wine nor to allow a razor to touch their heads. Thus the Nazirite's influence and example were undermined. To the prophets Israel said: "Prophesy not." This is the way the people treated the ambassadors of the God who had done so much for them. Israel did not persecute God's servants; no, they simply rendered them helpless. In a very "decent" and "civilized" way they silenced the word of God and did as they saw fit. They forgot the past. They live for "today."

What will be God's reaction to this attitude of his people? He sends Amos. Amos also is told not to prophesy (7:12-13) but he is not silenced. He is called to proclaim the judgment of God on the attitude which this people has manifested for a long time. The measure of Israel's iniquity is full. The punishment will not be turned away again.

Now the prophet comes with the word of judgment. "I will press you in your place as a cart presseth that is full of sheaves." There is a difference of opinion among commentators as to the exact meaning of these words. Yet, the explanation of the following verses depends on the

interpretation of these words. The most plausible
explanation seems to be the following: He will cause the
land to groan as a cart or wagon groans that is overloaded
with sheaves. The load is too heavy for the cart. As a result,
every movement causes it to groan. So will it be in Israel.
Israel. will be overloaded with the judgments of — God —
so that it will groan by reason of this burden. This includes
everything in Israel. Every institution, every movement,
their whole way of life will groan. God's judgments will
weigh heavily on the whole land.

No one will be able to escape this judgment of God.
The swift will not be able to flee it. The strength of the
strong man will not be sufficient to deliver him. No one will
be able to offer resistance. The bow will be a useless
weapon against the judgment of God. The horse is of no
help to deliver. No matter how courageous a man may be
he will have to flee away naked. There is no defense against
God's judgments!

These things are going to happen "in that day." That day
is spoken of again and again by the prophet. Israel looked
for the day of the Lord to be a glorious day. That day, they
believed, would mark their triumph. Amos reveals to them
the fact that that day will be the day of terror for the
enemies of God. The earthquake of which he spoke in the
beginning is a forerunner of that day.

Israel thought all was well until Amos came. They imagined
they were serving God and that God was favorably
disposed to them as was evident from the blessings which
he showered on them. Now they are told that they are
totally mistaken and that they have misinterpreted all the
signs. God is coming to judge their "innocent evils" and
their "splendid vices." They only sought to "tone down"
the message of the prophets and the strictness of the
Nazirites. These marred their festivities and disturbed their
sense of security. Compared to the surrounding nations,

Israel was a God-fearing people. Yet, the judgment is
pronounced. God does not compare Israel to the other
nations; he judges them in the light of his revelation.

This is God's warning to his people of every age.
Comparison with others is not the standard to be employed.
Favorable comparison with others does not justify us.
To the law and to the testimony!

Questions for Discussion

1. How can the knowledge of the past safeguard us against
   present-day sins? Of what value is the knowledge of
   church history?
2. How was the wilderness wandering of Israel a blessing
   for them?
3. Why was idolatry always such a temptation for Israel?
4. What was the place of the Nazirite in Israel's religion?
5. Is the church guilty of silencing the prophets today?
   If so, how?
6. When does a church arrive at the stage that it will no
   longer listen to the truth? Note: Where the truth is
   proclaimed the churches are filled, while most modernist
   churches are empty.

Divine Logic

Amos 3:1-8

God's logic is strange and has troubled people of every generation. Sometimes it does not follow the pattern of our logic at all. His thoughts are very deep. Again, that logic is very simple. A child can often understand it better than the wise.

The words which Amos now speaks are meant not only for Israel, but also for Judah. He addresses himself to the whole family which God delivered from Egyptian slavery. It has meaning for all of them. They are the only, ones whom he has known of all the families of the earth. This is, of course, not an intellectual knowledge. It is rather a "love-knowledge." He knew them intimately. He delivered them from Egypt and also bound them to himself with a covenant bond. It is as a marriage relationship. So had he not known any other people. What is now the conclusion which is to be drawn from this statement? Israel believes that he will conclude: therefore will I shower my blessings upon you. But, the divine logic answers in a different vein. Because I have *so* known you, therefore "I will visit upon you all your iniquities." Is that a strange conclusion? No! It hurts far more if a loved one turns against you than if a stranger does so.

The Lord now asks several questions. He does not give the answers because the answers are self-evident. These are simple questions. Though simple, they contain a wealth of thought. They are so simple that a child can answer them but his people seemingly do not know the answers. One has to live close to God to understand his logic.

Shall two walk together except they have agreed? Of course, the answer is, No. Two people do not fellowship together except there be basic agreement. Has it ever dawned on Israel that God will not walk with them if they are not in agreement with him? Will a lion roar in the forest when he hath no prey? Of course not. A lion roars when he is about to spring upon his prey. If he roars too soon, his prey will escape. When the lion is certain of his prey, when there is no possibility of escape, then he roars. God and Israel cannot walk together anymore. The judgment is now irrevocable. Will a young lion cry out of his den if he has taken nothing? Amos refers to a young lion, but one which already hunts. It has the prey and is already devouring it. The cry is one of satisfaction. Is there still a possibility of escape? To ask the question is to answer it.

There is a difference of opinion regarding the next question. We believe it to be as follows: Will a bird fall into a snare if he does not seek prey? The bird falls into the snare when he is tempted by its bait. Israel is tempted by the godless world. This will prove to be her undoing. Will a snare spring up from the earth if it has taken nothing? No, a bird falling on it only makes the snare jump up from the ground.

Shall the trumpet be blown in a city and the people not be afraid? The trumpet warns the people of approaching peril. When it sounds, the people tremble, but... Israel doesn't. The peril which approaches is the evil which Jehovah brings upon the city.

Amos further tells Israel that Jehovah will do nothing except he reveal his secret to the prophets. This does not mean that all the books of God are opened to the prophets so that every deed of his providence whereby he controls and governs the world is first made known to them. Rather, the great deeds of the Lord by which he brings about great changes in the history of his people, are first made known to the prophets. This should cause the people to listen intently to the message which the prophets bring because it comes directly from the mouth of Jehovah.

"The lion hath roared: who will not fear?" Amos is now drawing the conclusion of that which has gone before. His prophecy has been called "the gospel of the lion's roar." The lion does not roar until it is certain of its prey. The time is short. The lion has roared. The prey will naturally tremble. God's voice is now likened to the roar of a lion. That is not the way in which we are accustomed to speak of the voice of God. His voice is perfect. It is more beautiful than the voices of angels. But God also thunders and can also roar as a lion. He is angered against Israel. Against that people he utters his voice. Why doesn't the prey (Israel) freeze in fear? The logic of sinful Israel still sees no reason to fear.

When the Lord Jehovah speaks with such a voice, how shall anyone refrain from prophesying? That is the voice which Amos has heard. He *must* prophesy! There is no other way out. One can never forget such a roar! Compulsion is laid upon him. Amos is certainly not pictured as an emotional man. But this is more than he can stand. It is not a pleasant task to declare coming judgment to Israel, the people whom Amos loves. But, he must! How can anyone be silent when the lion's roar still sounds in his ears? One must be more than deaf not to hear it. Nor should the prophet be the only one who will prophesy. Everyone is to witness to it. Amos was not a professional prophet. He was a herdsman. But he was a herdsman who had heard the lion roar. How the lion roared in the history of Israel! How can this people be so complacent? How the lion roars in this 21st century! How can the church be at ease?

The lion's roar is heard in the wars of our lifetime. It is heard in the fears of the present time. Jehovah is speaking!

The trumpet is blowing; the lion is roaring; the snare is snapping shut; many are no longer walking in agreement with their God. How can one be silent under such conditions? Israel laughs at the prophet and continues its festivities. That is not logical. That is the logic of hell! This logic cries peace, peace... while the lion roars!

Questions for Discussion
1. God's thoughts are not our thoughts (Isaiah 55:8). Then how are we able to understand God?
2. Must one be learned to understand God's ways?
3. What are some of the lessons for today in the simple questions which are asked in this passage?
4. Should anyone become a minister unless he is constrained? Explain.
5. The voice of God is revealed in different ways in Scripture. Which voice heard the most in modern day preaching? Is this good or bad?
6. How does God speak to us today?
7. How can people be made to tremble at the word of God?

Lesson 8

Divine Irony

Amos 3:9-12

God employs various means to make his message clear to men. At times he will even use irony, a light sarcasm, to make his word unmistakably clear. We have only to think of Elijah's words to the prophets of Baal on Mount Carmel as an example. Amos uses this method very effectively at times.

Amos is here speaking to imaginary heralds. He tells them to go to Egypt and Ashdod (Philistia) to bring a message. They are to tell these heathen nations to come to Samaria. They should station themselves on the mountains around Samaria so that they may be able to see the things which the children of Israel do. They will stand amazed. Here they will learn something. Egypt had been the oppressor of Israel in early years. The cruelty of Egypt was great. A decree had gone out to slay all the male children of their slaves, the Israelites. Philistia had been Israel's oppressor several times after Israel had come to Canaan. Their cruelty was proverbial. Samson had been blinded by them and then compelled to work as an animal for them. But, if these nations want to know what real moral confusion and oppression is, let them come to Samaria! God's people have outdone the heathen!

When evil is committed by God's people, it is best that the matter should not be noised abroad. We should not give publicity to these things. But God tells these heralds to stand on the roofs of the palaces of these heathen lands and publish the evils found in Samaria. That is divine irony.

The world always looks closely at God's people. They

look critically at them. They expect more from them than from themselves. We are a "gazing stock." The world is often unfair in its evaluation of the lives of God's people. Yet God now tells them to look at them and see the evils which they have committed.

God's people know not to do right. This people, which has received the law and has been instructed as no other people, knows not the difference between right and wrong. Seemingly, all the instruction has been in vain. Violence and robbery are stored up in their palaces. They store it up as one would store up treasures. But Israel doesn't realize that it is walking the road to ruin. They are very religious and believe that all is well. Yes, Egypt and Ashdod should come and see what is going on in Israel. They will be shocked. Therefore it will also be more tolerable for them in the day of judgment than for the people of Israel.

In verse eleven the prophet speaks directly to Israel again. He speaks concerning the judgment which is coming upon the evils which he has described. An adversary, an enemy, is going to come. Who this enemy is he doesn't say. No doubt, this is a reference to Assyria. When this enemy comes, he is not going to sit on the mountains around Samaria and look, as Egypt and Ashdod are to do; he will go through the land to rid it of its evils. This enemy of Israel will be used as a servant of God to cleanse the land. Samaria's strength will be broken. The palaces, where violence and robbery had been stored up, will be plundered. This will be Israel's future, unless it repents.

In the concluding verse of this section Amos speaks of rescue. Is it beginning to dawn? Have his judgments and warnings been exhausted? Notice carefully the "rescue" of which he speaks. As a shepherd rescues two legs or a piece of an ear out of the mouth of a lion, so shall Israel be rescued. When a shepherd tears the lower parts of two legs or a piece of an ear out of a lion's mouth, we cannot say

that he has rescued or saved the sheep. No, these pieces are
evidence of the fact that the sheep has been devoured.
Why then bother about the two legs or the piece of an ear?
In Exodus 22:10-13 God had commanded the Israelites that
a shepherd should present evidence that an animal had been
torn by a wild beast. If no evidence was presented, there
would be the suspicion that the shepherd had stolen the
animal. So will Israel be rescued. It will be made evident to
all that the Shepherd has not been negligent. He has not
stolen. God is the Shepherd of his people. He has been
faithful. These two legs and piece of an ear are mute
testimony to that fact.

This "rescue" is not glorious. The tabernacle of David
falls (Amos 9:11). Only a "root" is left of the mighty tree
which God had planted. Only two legs and a piece of an ear
are left of the large flock of Israel. A remnant is left. This
remnant he rescues. In that remnant he has upheld his own
honor. From that remnant comes the "Good Shepherd."

The closing words of verse 12 are rather difficult to
translate. Here the prophet pictures the people who are to
be "rescued." They seem to be oblivious to the dangers
surrounding them. Do they still sit in their "easy chairs"
while the world is on fire? Apparently they do, according to
the common translation. Others (e.g. Van Gelderen) believe
that the preposition translated "in" should be translated
"with." Then the meaning becomes clear. As they are
"rescued" in the day the calamities come on Israel, they will
be found wandering about with a pillow or some other
piece of bedding. It will be with them as it was with the
refugees and displaced persons in Europe during the last
war. As they flee, they take the first thing they see. If they
have been awakened out of sleep, they will take pieces of
bedding. So they will wander about. So will they be rescued.

What a graphic description Amos gives of Israel's
judgment! As they listen to this man they can already

picture the things which are going to come. Amos warns. It is a warning to repent. How can anyone harden himself against such prophecy? Yet, Israel did!

Questions for Discussion
1. What should be our reaction when the world gazes at our lives and conduct critically?
2. When God's people fall into sin do they become greater sinners than the people of the world? If so, why?
3. How does God use the world to cleanse his church?
4. Who belong to the "remnant?"
5. What is the relationship between the term "remnant" and divine calling and election?

Lesson 9

Wealth and Judgment

Amos 3:13-4:3

Wealth has often been the undoing of both nations and
individuals. When used in the proper manner it can be a
great blessing but it is often used as an unrighteous power.
Israel enjoyed unheard of wealth in the days of Amos.
Although they had been warned against the pitfalls of
wealth again and again, they still fell into its snares.

God calls other peoples to testify against Israel. Israel had
received the fullest revelation but they did not listen to it.
Let other peoples, Ashdod and Egypt (vs. 9), now bring the
message to Israel. The content of this message is that God
will visit the transgression of Israel upon him. He will not
allow his sins to go unpunished. And when he visits these
transgressions, he will not only remove Israel's wealth; he
will also visit the altars of Bethel. The misuse of wealth is
but the symptom; the origin of the evil is to be found at the
altar. God goes to the heart of the matter. The false worship
of the people leads them to all manner of sins. The horns of
the altar, on which a fleeing person might lay hold for his
life, will be cut off and fall to the ground. There will be no
place of safety.

When the altars have been destroyed, God will attack the
exhibition of wealth. The wealthy in Israel have advanced
so far that they now have both summer and winter houses.
They can enjoy life to the full. Some have houses whose
walls are inlaid with ivory. Here is luxury. Not only the rich
but even the "common people" are enjoying wealth
unheard of before. To this the prophet refers when he

speaks of the "great," or rather the many, houses. But all of this wealth and luxury will come to an end. They have not been thankful in their prosperity. They have not used their wealth for the benefit of the needy. Their gold has become their god!

In the first verse of chapter four Amos uses a form of address which startles us. "Ye kine of Bashan." Is it right to address people this way? Isn't that going a little bit too far? Who are these kine, these cows of Bashan? The prophet refers to the women of Samaria! He likens them to the sleek, well-fed cogs that graze in the marvelous pastures of the land of Bashan to the east of the sea of Galilee. How these women must have hated this prophet for naming them the way he does! They must have concluded that Amos had lost all sense of decency. What a coarse and uncouth man!

Amos speaks the word of Jehovah. *God* calls those women "kine of Bashan." Why does the prophet censure *the women* so vehemently for this evil, in Israel? Women exert a great influence in any nation. Usually it is an influence which makes a nation more humane. They often have more tender feeling and compassion for those in need. But if the women of a nation have become evil so that they deserve the name "cows of Bashan" there is little hope that justice will be given to the poor. This was the situation in Israel.

They say to their husbands, "Bring, and let us drink." When their husbands leave the house in the morning their women urge them to make money so that they may continue their manner of life. More is needed every day. The wives call their husbands "lords," reminding us of the relationship of Sarah and Abraham. However, the resemblance is only one of words. Their husbands have become their slaves! They are so accustomed to the life of luxury that it must continue at all costs. Their luxury is bought at the expense of the poor. Amos tells them that they have oppressed the poor and have crushed the needy. Their insatiability wrought havoc in the lives of the poor. Indeed, they are like the sleek, well-fed cows of Bashan who seek only their own comfort. They have neither mercy nor compassion for the needy.

God will not allow the wickedness portrayed in the first verse to go unpunished. He has sent his prophet to warn them. Oh, that they may yet turn from their evil ways! If they will not turn, the punishment will certainly come. The Lord swears by his holiness that they will not escape. His holiness is the standard by which human conduct will be judged. No arbitrary standard is used.

The manner of their punishment is again pictured very vividly. They had been likened to the cows of Bashan. Now Amos likens them to the fishes of the sea. Surely, he does not come with flattering words to the women of Samaria. They may be shocked by the words he uses, but no one will criticize this prophet for being vague! He is not afraid to use very plain language.

Destruction is going to come upon the women of Samaria as it comes to the fishes of the sea. They swim about in their true element. Suddenly they see food dangled before them. A fish, of course, does not realize that this food contains the deadly hook. In its greed it bites into the bait and is caught by the hook it contains. So will destruction come to the women of Samaria. They are never satisfied. Tomorrow must yield more than today if they are going to be successful. They will finally eat their death in their wealth. Death-dealing judgment is concealed in their wealth. All of them will be taken. There will be none remaining.

That the destruction will be complete is further pictured in verse three. They will go out at the breaches, everyone straight before her. The whole wall will be broken down. The walls which were designed to give protection will be destroyed as completely as the walls of Jericho in the days of Joshua. Every man could go straight before him; no part of the wall barred his way (Joshua 6:20). Their whole world in which they trusted will come tumbling down. So they will go into captivity to another land, here called Harmon.

How their glory has departed! All because of the misuse of wealth! But these things were also written for our admonition, upon whom the ends of the ages are come!

Questions for Discussion
1. What are some of the dangers for us in these prosperous times?
2. How does the "altar" influence the lives of the people?
3. What was the importance of the horns of the altar?
4. How can the women of a nation be an influence for good or evil?
5. Is it wrong to have both a summer and winter house? Is it wrong to have elaborate houses if one can afford them?
6. Can God's judgments ever be too severe? Explain.

Lesson 10

Sinful Worship

Amos 4:4-5

Israel had made itself guilty of many sins. Amos is, sent to
the house of Israel to warn them that God's judgments will
certainly come upon them for these sins. Israel was shocked
that the picture drawn by the prophet should be so dark.
They were religious people. They kept the law. They prided
themselves on their ancestry. They were far different from
the other nations.

Amos had referred to the reason for the evils in Israel
before. Though they are religious, their religion is not pure.
The heart is nor right with Jehovah. They worship, but they
do not worship as he has commanded. Their religion is
man-made. No matter how religious they may be, it does
not find favor with their God; it opens the way to all
manner of sinful practices. If one's religion is not genuine,
very little good can be expected of his walk of life.

The prophet uses bitter irony in these two verses. Come to
Bethel and transgress and to Gilgal to multiply
transgressions! These were the places where Israel
worshiped. Should not the prophet be pleased that these
people bring their sacrifices? The prophets had often been
sent to urge the people to sacrifice. Israel now. brings
sacrifices and the prophet criticizes them for doing it. He is
never satisfied! The people bring even more than is
required. They are zealous.

Where do they worship? Why, at Bethel and Gilgal, of
course. Bethel was the place where Jacob had seen the
angels of God. God had appeared to him there. Later Jacob

had been commanded to erect an altar there (Gen. 35:1). This was a holy place. Jeroboam I had, very naturally, chosen Bethel as one of the places where Israel might come to worship. Gilgal was also an important place in the history of God's people. There Israel had encamped when they crossed the Jordan into Canaan. There the stones had been set up as a memorial to God's wonderful deliverance of his people. No, their places of worship were not chosen haphazardly. They were very carefully chosen. Surely, Israel can not go to Jerusalem to worship. That city is in Judah! Besides, at Jerusalem it is all tradition. The worship is so cold. Here at Bethel and Gilgal they feel at home.

In God's sight the place of worship was not an insignificant matter. Jerusalem had been chosen by himself as the place where Israel was to worship. Regardless of the history of other places or the circumstances which made it difficult to go there, Jerusalem was the place! They sin in "coming" to Bethel and Gilgal. They had dedicated these places as places of worship, but they would not find Jehovah there.

They do not only sin in coming to worship at the places which God had not chosen; they also sin in their manner of worship. Israel looks the part of the cheerful and liberal giver at both Bethel and Gilgal. However, the prophet is not blinded by the number or value of the offerings. They bring their sacrifices every morning. There is nothing wrong with that. They bring their tithes (the third day?) regularly. They also offer a sacrifice of thanksgiving of that which is leavened. Besides the unleavened bread, they also sacrifice that which was not demanded. Free-will offerings are brought besides all this. These offerings are "published" so that everyone may be aware of their religious zeal. They go beyond the demands of the law. These people are indeed religious! If one gives so liberally is it not usually a sign of real spirituality? These people do not only speak of their religion with the mouth, they also practice it at the altar.

Yet, in spite of it all, the prophet speaks his woes over this people.

Why is the prophet not pleased with their exhibition of spirituality? Because real spirituality is totally lacking! Amos is sent by Him who looks on the heart of man. Despite all their sacrifices, the hearts of this people are still far removed from him. Externally all was in order. Within their hearts everything was wrong. The people who brought their many offerings at Bethel and Gilgal were the same people who oppressed the poor and crushed the needy. The multitude of their offerings had to serve to cover up their social sins. If the smoke of the altar became thick enough, they might not be able to see the misery of the poor. If they would sing their Psalms loudly enough, they might be able to drown out the cry of the oppressed.

The manner of Israel's Old Testament worship revealed many dangers. The altar was the center of their worship. The law prescribed the various offerings to be brought. It was so easy to live up to all the demands of the law and still engage in sinful worship. The prophets were sent again and again to warn the people that their God demanded more than the blood of bulls and goats. The heart, the attitude, of the worshipper was the important thing. Then only would the sacrifice be acceptable if it were brought with a believing heart. These dangers have not disappeared with the removal of the altar.

The prophet uses sarcasm in speaking to Israel concerning its sinful worship. "Come to Bethel... come to Gilgal." Go ahead! Keep it up! Of course, he does not urge the people to keep on sinning. This manner of speaking is intended to show them the evil of their ways most clearly. They believe that they are observing all that which Jehovah commanded them. If they go on in this way, it will lead them to ruin!

Why do the Israelites still practice their religious rites if their hearts are not in it? Essentially, it is to please themselves. *That* is the heart of their religion. It is not to please God but themselves. Regardless of the fact that he has chosen Jerusalem, they will worship at Bethel and Gilgal! Although he demands much more than numbers of sacrifices, they bring these sacrifices and believe that all will then be well. The place, the manner, the purpose... all is sinful! No blessing will attend such worship.

Questions for Discussion

1. Calvinism stresses the influence of religion for all of life. Why is this not so apparent among others?
2. Why was the place of worship so important? Is this still true?
3. How only can our gifts be an expression of true spirituality?
4. Was there more danger of externalism in Israel's religion than in ours? Explain.
5. If the heart is right do externals still matter?

Lesson 11

Unrepentant Israel

Amos 4:6-11

All of God's dealings with his people throughout their history were for the purpose of drawing them closer to him. If his people sin, he calls them to repent. When they repent he forgives. The unrepentant can never enjoy the favor of God.

God uses various means to call his people to repentance. In this section he speaks of calamities that were sent to call the people back to God. The question naturally arises: Were these past calamities or was this a prophecy of future woes? Amos prophesied during prosperous times. Yet, though the times were now prosperous, calamities have come during the lifetime of the people to whom he is speaking, or in the times of their fathers. David, too, ruled in prosperous times but there was also a three-year famine during his reign (II Sam. 21:1). The calamities have come, but now they are past. Prosperity is seen everywhere and they have forgotten the days of calamity.

God has given the people cleanness of teeth. This was a judgment. They had cleanness of teeth because there was lack of bread. Their teeth remained clean because no food entered their mouth. God did this to them! This fact they may never forget. He often uses means to bring his judgments, but he brings them! A "scientific" explanation for the evils which come can never satisfy God's people. In this instance too he had used means. He simply withheld the rain. When there were still three months before the harvest the rains ceased. Under such conditions there could

be no harvest in Palestine. Notice, he could make it rain at
will. He is in control of the forces of nature. This he makes
very clear to his people. He caused it to rain on one city,
but not on another. One piece of land did receive rain, but
not the other. Where the rain did not fall everything withered.

  Lack of rain does not only produce famine, it also does
more. If nothing grows there may still be a surplus from
previous years. But when no rain falls it also produces
thirst. The effect of this is immediate. Two or three cities go
to another for water. The city to which they go is one where
the rain has fallen. Here there may be sufficient water for
its own inhabitants, but there is not enough to satisfy the
needs of two or three other cities. Even though some cities
have not felt the immediate effects of the general famine,
they now suffer want because they must share their water
with neighbors.

  Although the lack of rain would produce famine and
untold misery for many people, God has sent more woes on
the land. Blasting and mildew, crop diseases had come at
various times. Even though crops grew, they could not be
used. Palmer worms devoured trees and vines. All these
evils had come on Israel at different times during their
history. They must always remember that God sent
these things.

  There have also been times of pestilence. This pestilence
may have been on both man and beast. So Egypt had also
suffered at the time of the plagues. These pestilences
claimed many lives. Those were the days when medical
science was not able to stop the onward march of pestilence
and disease. Whole cities and districts might be
depopulated. God sent these woes!

  War has taken its toll. The young men, the best of the
nation, were slain by the sword. Their horses fell prey to
the enemy. Their camps have been destroyed. These were
times of bitter wailing! How God has chastised his people!

Whole cities had been overthrown, had been dashed to the ground, as Sodom and Gomorrah had been destroyed. Here the reference is not to war but rather to earthquakes. These natural calamities were not unknown in Palestine. When these earthquakes came to destroy whole cities, those who escaped were as brands plucked out of the fire. They had suffered, they had been scorched, but their lives had been saved. These people were like Lot. He also escaped the destruction of the cities of the plain, but he did not escape unscathed. God had also brought this calamity on the land.

After the reference to each calamity the prophet adds the refrain: "Yet have ye not returned unto me, saith Jehovah." *That* was the purpose of these woes! He was seeking his people! Better that they suffer the physical and temporal evils than that they should live and die separated from their God. How can a people be so hardened that they will not turn to their God when such woes strike? God sought their *conversion.* That is the word which the prophet uses in this refrain. Conversion is a return to the living God. But Israel has not done so. One blow fell after the other, but they did not return to God. Didn't they realize that it was his hand which struck these blows? No doubt, the people often spoke of the heavy hand of God upon them while one of these calamities lasted. But, that isn't *conversion!* They never returned *all the way* to God. He spoke through the prophets, but he also spoke through his deeds. What else must he do to cause this people to return to him? One marvels that God does not weary of speaking to such a people.

As we said before, the book of Amos could have been written yesterday. Within the span of one human life many calamities have come. World War I, the most severe economic depression in modern times, World War II, and the Korean war, have all come in a short period of time. Besides these, God has also sent great prosperity, whereby he speaks to his people too. What has been the result?

Has the man of today learned from the experiences of the people of Amos' day? Scientific reasons are found for many of the ills which have come. No, *God* sent them! His hand rules all. Despite all the calamities suffered in recent history, the somber refrain of Amos applies to the people of today as well as to the people 2800 years ago: "Yet have ye not returned unto me, saith Jehovah." That is tragic!

Questions for Discussion

1. What is the relationship between "scientific reasons" and the hand of Jehovah?
2. Why must we see the hand of God in all the minor things of life?
3. What is conversion? What is the difference between conversion and regeneration?
4. Is man responsible for his own conversion?
5. Why do the deeds of God usually make a deeper impression than his word?

Lesson 12

Judgment on the Unrepentant

Amos 4:12-13

God has visited Israel with many judgments in the past.
These were sent to induce Israel to repent. Even though the
people had suffered greatly, none of these woes led to
repentance. Now what? Will he leave them where they are?
Will he now cast off his people? Men would judge that he
had gone far enough. This people is not worthy of further
attention. But God does not judge according to man's
standards. Mercy is not forgotten even in his judgments.

Because Israel would not listen to previous judgments,
God will now use different tactics. "Ye have not returned
unto me... therefore thus will I do unto thee, O Israel." The
question immediately arises, What will he now do to them?
The previous judgments were clearly described.
Now he will do "thus" unto them.

To say the least, this is vague. In fact, he doesn't say at all
what he is going to do to them. Israel is left in the dark.
We are here reminded of the formula of the oath as it was
employed in Old Testament times: "God do so to me and
more also." This was also a very indefinite statement.
Why does God speak to Israel in this way? Surely, he has a
judgment in mind which will be more terrible than all those
which have gone before. Why does he not tell them what
that judgment will be? He speaks as he does to instill fear in
the hearts of his people. The third commandment is similar
in its wording. "Jehovah will not hold him guiltless that
taketh his name in vain." He does not say *how* he will
punish, but the individual will not be held guiltless. So God

now warns Israel. Former calamities have not had the
desired effect, but this judgment will be decisive.

How will Israel be able to prepare itself to meet this
coming calamity? It is so vague, so indefinite. They know
not what is coming. God gives the answer. None of the
other calamities caused them to return to God. Now,
because he will do *this* to them, they must prepare to meet
him. They will not be able to avoid this meeting.

The words "Prepare to meet thy God" have been
interpreted and applied in various ways. We may never do
violence to the context in which these words appear.
The context determines the interpretation and the scope
of the application.

Israel's meeting with God is inevitable. Nothing will
prevent this meeting. They must therefore prepare for it.
Will they be able to stand before him when they are
summoned? They should look at this very carefully. Will
they meet him as their equal? Will it be like the meeting of
one man with another? They should consider this. If it will
not be that kind of meeting, but rather a meeting with one
who stands far above them, then they should prepare
themselves as one who is to meet his judge. He is speaking
to Israel, to the people whom he has chosen. This people
will meet him. As they prepare for this meeting they must
look within. They are to come in penitence. If the breach
between God and his people is to be healed they will have
to meet. This meeting with God will be the end for the
unrepentant. But in that meeting there is life for those who
come in penitence. In the following chapter Amos speaks of
seeking Jehovah in order to live (Amos 5:4, 6, 14). He will
not continue to send judgments to which the people will
react as they please. The die is cast. He will summon them
to appear before him. How he will summon them is left
undefined, but the fact is certain. Now, then, prepare for
that meeting! He still warns — he gives them time.

The last verse of this chapter is a doxology. However, it is not a doxology which has no connection with the previous thought. Israel is called to prepare to meet its God. That preparation will be determined by the nature of their God. Who is he? To that question he gives an answer in this verse.

Their God is the almighty Creator of heaven and earth. He it is who formed the mountains and created the wind. This is the God whom they are to meet. Man was to have dominion over all things. He was to subdue the earth. Man has made giant strides in this direction. His success has often blinded him to the fact that he is still a dependent creature. Regardless how much man may have accomplished, God is infinitely greater. He made the mountains! Man uses the wind, God created it. Let Israel never give place to the mistaken notion that it can meet God as an equal.

Not only is God the almighty Creator; he also declares to man his thoughts. God knows the thoughts which man has never expressed. He was able to see whether or not Israel's worship was genuine. They cannot stand before him with excuses. He will therefore also be the perfect Judge when they meet him. Nothing will be hidden from him. Man knows much. His knowledge increases constantly. But God knows everything! There is no comparison. Let them prepare to meet this God of infinite knowledge.

God makes the morning darkness. That is the reverse of the natural order. The morning dispels the darkness. Here the prophet refers to the storm clouds which God forms to hide the light. When these storm clouds gather, man trembles. He stands helpless before these powers of nature. But God treads upon the high places of the earth. He makes the storm clouds. He then walks majestically on them as though they were a carpet.

This is Jehovah, the God of hosts! He has control over all the universe. This is the God whom they are to meet!

Careful preparation is required. He summons them. He will still speak to them. He had previously overthrown some of their cities as Sodom and Gomorrah had been overthrown. Sodom did not repent — neither did Israel. However, Sodom's overthrow was the end; Israel is still called to meet its God. Prepare to meet him, for why will ye die, O house of Israel?

Questions for Discussion
1. Why didn't God always inform the people what the particular judgment was going to be?
2. Are the words "Prepare to meet thy God" a fit text for preparatory services? Give reasons.
3. What is meant by the common phrase that we must **always** be prepared? What does this involve? Is it possible?
4. Does man's greater knowledge of the universe usually bring him closer to God or not? Why?
5. Can the thought of the greatness of God lead to penitence? Is general revelation a good avenue of approach to the unbeliever?

The Urgency of Seeking Jehovah

Amos 5:1-17

This part of the "sermon" of the prophet Amos does not run very smoothly. Woes are pronounced and invitations to seek Jehovah are extended. However, this is not a weakness but something to be expected of a prophet whose heart is burdened with the sad condition of the people whom he loves. Reasoning must make way for the unburdening of a pastoral heart.

Amos calls the people to listen to a lamentation, a funeral dirge, over themselves. They are very much alive and believe that all is well with them. Now this prophet begins to sing this funeral dirge! To listen to the songs sung at one's own funeral; to look into one's own coffin — how gruesome! Yet, that is exactly what Amos means. He sees the virgin of Israel (the people of Israel) as already dead. None shall raise her up. Formerly the armies of Israel went forth as tribes, but in Amos' day they go out by cities. The city which sends forth a thousand men into battle will see only one hundred return. Similarly, where a hundred are sent out, only ten will return. This means complete defeat. God himself has prophesied this.

Because their defeat will be total if they continue in the way they are going, Amos calls them to seek Jehovah. Then they will live. This is the only way out. Certain destruction awaits their present mode of life while the fullness of life is promised them if they seek Jehovah. Surely, that choice should not be difficult! But then they must not go to Gilgal or Bethel or Beersheba. Jehovah will not be found there. No, these places themselves will go into captivity. These were places of historic importance, but that does not save. Seek *him*! One can go to a place of worship and still not seek God. Living union must be established.

If they will not seek Jehovah, he will break out like a fire on the house of Israel. Jehovah will save them if they seek him but this same God will consume them if they don't seek him. Surely, there is sufficient reason for his anger to be poured out on them. Justice has been turned to wormwood. Bitterness has taken the place of that which was to be sweet. Righteousness is forgotten and is trampled under foot.

Who is the God whom they are to seek? He is Jehovah, their covenant God. He is also the Almighty Creator. He has made the constellations in the heavens. He governs all things. He turns the day into night. He causes vapors to ascend to form clouds which bring rain on the earth. Here we hear a doxology. Amos sings the praises of the Almighty. No one will be able to stand before this God. Strength cannot save the strong, neither is a fortress adequate protection. This is the God whom they must seek. He is able to defend them and give life.

How far the decay of morality had progressed in Israel is stated very clearly. Those who still raise their voices against evil are hated by the people. They detest those who speak uprightly. They wish to pursue their evil ways unhindered. The poor, whose rights were guaranteed by the law, are trampled under foot. Israel was not permitted to exact interest on loans to their brethren. Formally the people still obey this law. However, those who had received loans were now forced to bring grain besides the repayment of the loan. In this way the lenders still received interest. Oh, this people has become wealthy. Once only kings' palaces were built of hewn stone, but now the wealthy merchants in Israel

can afford them. However, though they build such houses,
they will not enjoy them. Though they plant vineyards, they
will not enjoy the fruit. God will intervene. He knows their
sin. Sins which have been committed in secret are well
known to him. Punishment will surely come if they continue
this practice. The days are so evil that a prudent and wise
man will keep silence. Only money talks in Israel in Amos'
day. The words of the wise are drowned out. No, it is never
good when the wise keep silent. They should protest against
the evil of their day regardless of the hope of success. But
Amos is here merely characterizing the day in which he lives.
The wise have given up all hope. Now only the word of the
foolish is heard. Indeed this is an evil time.

Although the prudent man may keep silence, Jehovah does
not. He pleads, by the mouth of the prophet, to seek him,
to seek the good. The people are always speaking of the
blessings of God upon them. They say: God is with us —
witness the blessings he has given. That is not true! Only if
they will seek the good, will Jehovah be with them. Then
they will live. This seeking of the good is not something
vague but is very definite and very positive. They must love
the good — then they will seek it. They must hate the evil
— then will they flee it. That goodness is to consist of
justice performed in the gate. As long as there is no justice
between a man and his brother all their religious exercises
are of no avail. Evil has already claimed many, but by
turning to Jehovah a remnant of Israel may still be spared.
The matter is urgent. If they do not turn, all Israel will
be destroyed.

Once more the prophet pictures the result if they will not
give heed to the word he has spoken. Their God is still
speaking to them. He urges repentance. He warns. There
will be wailing in all the principal streets. A great cry is sure
to go up from the whole land. It will be a cry of despair.
Utter misery is pictured. People will be able to say nothing

but "Alas, alas!" Farmers will be called in from the fields to mourn. Hired mourners will go about the streets. There will be wailing in the vineyards. The only sound heard in the land will be the sound of mourning. All this misery will be produced because God is going to go through the land. He will visit with his judgments. Then it will be too late. This is the same God who urges the people to turn to him. If they turn to him in time they will find that he alone gives true life. If they will not turn they will find that he brings complete destruction. The choice is very simple. It is still the same today.

Questions for Discussion

1. What do you think of Amos' psychology in urging repentance?
2. What does the mention of Beersheba teach us about Israel's argument that they should not go to Jerusalem to worship because it was in Judah?
3. Will not the description of the Almighty Creator frighten people? What other doctrine must always be made clear in this same connection? See Lord's Day 9.
4. How were the rights of the poor safeguarded by the Mosaic law? Could there ever be poverty in Israel if they obeyed the law? Why will we always have the poor with us?
5. Why must we always protest against evil even when we can see that it will do no good?
6. Isn't it quite sure whether Jehovah will save those who turn to him (vs. 15)?

Lesson 14

The Day of Jehovah

Amos 5:18-27

Israel always looked longingly for the great day of Jehovah to come. That would be the great day in which God's people would be justified. Regardless what men might think of them or do to them, God would vindicate their honor on that day. Especially in times of distress this longing would be very pronounced. In New Testament times we have something similar. The prayer for the return of Jesus is never stronger than in the days of persecution. Evil will be vanquished and the right will triumph on the day of Jehovah.

In the days of Amos the people of Israel also longed for the day of Jehovah to make its appearance. True, it was a time of prosperity. Yet, Israel considered the day of Jehovah to be so much better than their own days that they hoped it would soon come. This seemed to be an indication of a high spiritual level.

The prophet Amos, however, does not consider this desire to be an indication of true spirituality, but of gross ignorance. What will the day of Jehovah be like? That day will not come, first of all, to vindicate the honor of the people, but rather to vindicate the honor of God! Woe to the sinners on that day! For the sinners it will be a day of darkness and not light. Israel's sins have been described. For Israel it will be a day of darkness unless they repent. The day of Jehovah will be the blackest of days for the unrepentant.

The description which Amos gives of that day for unrepentant Israel is very vivid. He pictures a man fleeing for his life and not able to escape. A man is being pursued by a lion. He flees for his life and finally escapes the lion's jaws. However, when he has left the lion behind him he meets a bear. His life is again endangered. Again he must flee. He succeeds in eluding the bear and comes to a hunter's hut in the forest. Being wearied because of his flight from the lion and bear, he leans his hand against the wall of the hut. Has he escaped danger? No, for as he leans his hand against the wall, a small serpent, hidden in a crack of the wall, bites his hand and sends its deadly venom into his blood stream. There is no escape. So shall it be on the day of Jehovah. It will be a very dark day without any brightness. Surely, only those who do not understand will long for that day to come.

Will that day not be a day of light for the people of God? Most certainly. Does Israel not reveal itself as a very religious people? Is the worship of God not central in their lives?

The churches, so to speak, are filled to overflowing in Israel. The people contribute liberally. The songs of Zion are heard everywhere. Music, dedicated to the praise of God, fills their temples.

What does the prophet have to say about the religious fervor in Israel? He says: God despises your feasts and doesn't care for your assemblies. Not all worship is good. A church full of people is not necessarily an indication of spiritual life. God even *hates* these feasts. They bring their sacrifices as God commanded, but he will not accept them. Their singing is judged to be *noise*. He doesn't care for their instrumental music. What's wrong? Is he never satisfied? They have been zealous in observing all his laws regarding worship. Now he doesn't want it!

The simple answer to all the questions which may arise in the minds of the Israelites is that they have done one thing commanded them but have neglected that which was more important. Justice and righteousness have been neglected. No amount of sacrifices will cover this neglect. As long as this situation is not remedied their religious exercises are of no use — they are sin. Justice should roll down as waters. Righteousness should flow as a never-drying stream. When these things have regained their rightful place, their offerings will be acceptable and the day of Jehovah will be light.

How important are the sacrifices? Of course, they may not be neglected. But when Israel looks back into its own history, which it loves to do, they will discover that there were times when sacrifices were not brought. Amos refers to the years spent in the wilderness. No doubt some sacrifices were brought at that time, but it was impossible for them to bring all the sacrifices prescribed by law. Even the sacrament of circumcision had been neglected (Joshua 5:5-7). Amos does not now consider their responsibility in regard to this matter. However, sacrifices have not always been brought, but justice and righteousness are always demanded.

Verse 26 is difficult to translate properly. The translation we have points to the past. They have, in the past, borne the tabernacle of their king and the shrine of their gods. This is not correct. They *will* bear these things. The tense here is future. Israel worships Jehovah but it also worships idols. They put a measure of trust in these idols. The idols referred to are the gods of the Babylonians. These gods will not be able to give help in the day of Jehovah. These gods too will be borne into captivity, for they are no gods.

Because of all the evil found in the house of Israel, the people will go into captivity beyond Damascus, to the realm of Assyria. What a disappointment! They were longing for the day of Jehovah to come when all their enemies would be defeated and they would enjoy the fullness of life. Instead, their enemies will take them captive. The enemy will triumph and they will be defeated. This day of Jehovah is certainly dark!

Appearances can be deceiving. Everything looked favorable in Israel. But he who sends the day of Jehovah is the God who looks within the heart of man. There he finds only evil. The forms of godliness are maintained, but its power is broken. God demands justice and righteousness. Obedience is still better than sacrifice.

Questions for Discussion
1. What was the significance of the "day of Jehovah?"
2. Why will that day be darker than others for the ungodly?
3. Does our church life today reveal a deep piety? Discuss.
4. Was Israel punished for its neglect of sacrifice in the wilderness?
5. How could Israel still serve idols in the light of all the revelation they had received? Have we escaped this sin?
6. Should God's people long for the "day of Jehovah?"

Lesson 15

False Optimism

Amos 6:1-6

The messages of woe are rather common in the book of
Amos. This prophet is speaking to a people which does not
realize its own danger. Despite the frequency of the woes,
there is nothing monotonous in the message of this farmer-
prophet of Tekoa.

In this section Amos pronounces his woes on those who
are at ease in both Jerusalem and Samaria. They enjoy the
present and are very optimistic in regard to the future.
They feel perfectly secure. How will anyone be able to take
the fortress of Zion? Jerusalem is surrounded by mountains.
Samaria has been made a fortified city. No harm will ever
touch the inhabitants of these strongholds.

Those who have this view of the matter are the notable
and chief men. They are the rulers and judges. All the
leaders feel secure. And, certainly, these are the people who
understand the times better than others. They are at ease.
They enjoy themselves.

Go to the surrounding nations. Go to the ancient city of
Calneh. Go to the great Hamath. Go to the city of the
giants in Philistia. Are these nations stronger than ours?
Is their area as great as ours? The implied answer is: No!
Israel is larger and more powerful than any of the places
named. Of course, the prophet is rather selective in his
choice of places for comparison. The glory of these places
has departed. Israel seems to be strong when compared with
them. If Israel were compared to some of the other
surrounding nations she would not appear in such favorable

light. When a reason has to be given for optimism, comparisons can be found which will make everything look good. Amos is again using irony.

The evil day is placed far into the future. If evil will befall the land it is so far off that no one will need to worry. It may come, of course. Yet, one need not now be alarmed because it cannot come as long as present conditions obtain!

But, says Amos, you are already paving the way for evil to overtake you. The seat of violence is found in Israel. The very people who are crying Peace, Peace, are the ones who are determining the destruction of the land.

These are the people who are enjoying themselves to the extreme. Their luxury has lulled them into a feeling of false security. They lie on beds inlaid with ivory. What wealth! What luxury! Formerly the people sat at tables to eat (I Samuel 20:24, I Kings 13:20) but now they recline. They "sprawl" on their couches — another indication of leisure and complete confidence in their safety. They eat the very best. The shepherd's heart of the prophet must have bled when he spoke these words. They eat the lambs and the calves. The food formerly reserved for kings is now the food of all the notables.

While they are feasting they must also have the atmosphere which surrounds such occasions. They sing idle songs. Not the praises of their God, but, as we would say today, jazz! David had made instruments of music. These people are not one whit behind the sweet singer of Israel. They, too, invent musical instruments. Amos points to these "instruments" with scorn. They are the kind of instruments one needs to accompany idle songs. With the music comes the wine. The prophet has, however, more to say about the vessels from which they drink the wine than about the wine itself. They drank from bowls, large containers. These were bowls used in worship. In their hilarity they do virtually the same as a later king of Babylon, Belshazzar. One more characteristic of their feasting must be named to make the picture complete. They anoint themselves with the chief oils. The hall of feasting is perfumed with the smell of the best oil. This oil was also, no doubt, used in their worship. These people certainly are pictured as being at ease. They deny themselves no enjoyment. Revelry and hilarity are found among those who are to lead, to give direction.

The prophet is dismayed at this picture of frivolity. These leaders are not grieved for the affliction of Joseph. The land of Israel is decaying. Joseph is afflicted. Israel's decay is certain to bring ruin. That fact ought to receive the attention of these principal men. Instead of feasting, they should be attired in sackcloth. They should do their utmost to uproot the evil and to turn Israel back to its God. But they are not grieved. To point out the evil which exists in the land is very unpopular. Let it go! Let us have a good time while we can! But this will be their undoing.

No wonder the prophet introduces this section by saying: "Woe to them that are at ease in Zion... and in Samaria." How can anyone be at ease when destruction threatens? How can one who knows the conditions feast at such a time? No one in his right mind can do that. But that is exactly the point: sin robs one of his understanding. Satan anesthetizes his victims.

This word has been preserved for the benefit of God's people of every age. The church, as long as she is on earth, is to be a militant church. Woe, therefore, to those who are at ease! Zion and ease are opposites! The church and ease are opposites! As soon as Zion is at ease, the destruction is at the door.

Despite this warning against false optimism, Israel persisted in that error. Despite all the warnings of Scripture anent this evil, the church has fallen into this error again and again. Ease is much more appealing than militancy. Feasting is much more attractive than sackcloth. Reasons for optimism can always be found, especially if one is selective in the comparisons he makes. This false optimism, this ease, is perhaps one of the greatest dangers which confronts the church in any age.

Questions for Discussion

1. Why is the feeling of security one of the greatest evils which can befall the people of God?
2. Why is it that great prosperity and luxurious living often precede the downfall of a nation?
3. Can music be immoral? Is jazz immoral?
4. Was it evil to use items intended to be used in **false** worship for their own pleasures?
5. What attitude toward the people did this false optimism of their leaders display? Do you think there is such false optimism in the church today?
6. What is meant by the term "militant church?" In how far must the church be militant?

When the Day Comes!

Amos 6:7-14

The second main division of the book of Amos, from 3:1 to 6:14, contains the various prophecies which the prophet has spoken to the people of his day. They have been messages of woe for their sins. The sins of Israel were vividly portrayed. The people must first know how great their sins and miseries are. The people have prided themselves on their wealth. They give an outward impression of real piety. They have expressed their longing for the great day of Jehovah to come.

What is it going to be like when that great day does come? Amos had already warned them that it would be a day of darkness and not light (5:18). Now that day will be described more fully.

The individuals to whom he has addressed himself specifically at the beginning of this chapter are the notable men. These were the "first" among the "first" people. How will they be "first?" They will be the first to go captive! These people who lay sprawled on their couches doing wickedness will be taken out of their own land. God will remove the revelry by removing those who practice it. Jehovah has been patient with this nation, but the measure of iniquity is full to overflowing. He abhors the pride of Israel. Their pride has blinded their eyes to their own sin. He now hates Israel's palaces. No longer does Jehovah delight in his people. He has sworn by himself to deliver up the whole city (Samaria) and all it contains. There is no possibility of reprieve. When God swears by himself it is certain. When men bolster their words with an oath, the

truth of something extremely important is established.
When God swears by himself, absolute certainty is
established. He swears that Israel will go into captivity.

To give as clear a picture as possible of that day which is
coming, the prophet now gives an illustration of what will
happen. In this illustration the people will have a picture of
that day of Jehovah. The prophet does not speak
concerning the darkness of that day in general terms only.
He is very specific. This is the picture: Even though there
may be ten persons in one house, in one family, they will all
die. Not only will the sword of the enemy slay, but
pestilence will also claim its victims. When death has come
to the inhabitants of this house, a relative will come with
one who will take the bodies for cremation. Cremation is
evil (2:1) but the times are such as to make this method of
disposing of dead bodies necessary. While the bodies are
being removed, the relative hears someone in a back room
of the house. Here is one who is sick and still living.
The relative calls to him and asks if there are any others
with him. The answer is: No. He then cautions the sick man
not to say any more. There is a danger that he will speak
the name of Jehovah in these circumstances. The Israelites
spoke that name so readily. Especially now, in this time of
unspeakable grief, there is the danger that Jehovah's name
will be spoken. Danger? Would this not be natural? Would
it also not be desirable to hear the name of the God of life
here in the midst of death?

Here Amos shows the thinking of the people of Israel.
It was similar to the thinking of the heathen. The heathen
believed, and Israel now shares that view, that if the name
of a deity were mentioned, his attention would be attracted!
Don't mention the name of Jehovah! He is the One who has
caused this evil to come. If you now mention his name, you
will attract his attention, and you and I who are still living
will also perish. They have become afraid of Jehovah!

This is not a godly fear, but a fear born of heathen superstition. Amos illustrates the conditions of that day and their religious thinking.

The people have not been mistaken in the view that it is indeed Jehovah who has brought this evil upon them. He commands the evil to come. He has jurisdiction over all powers. Both the great house and the little house shall be smitten. Amos is not a revolutionary who hurls his woes only against the rich. The sins of Israel are found among all classes. The rich may have greater opportunities to sin but the poor are no better.

Do horses run upon the rocks? Do unshod horses run on sharp stones? Of course not. Will one plow with oxen? The answer is: Yes. We see, therefore, that this is a meaningless translation. The prophet expects the same answer in both instances. The translation favored by the best scholars is: Will one plow *the sea* with oxen? Then the answer must be: No. Amos here speaks of impossible things No horse would run on jagged rocks. No one would ever think of plowing the sea with oxen. Natural laws are readily understood by men. But Israel has turned justice into poison and the result of righteousness into something bitter. This practice of Israel in the moral realm is no more logical than horses running on rocks or plowing the sea with oxen in the physical realm.

Verse 13 is also very difficult to understand in our translation. Two names are mentioned in the original which we do well to leave untranslated. These are names of places, Lodebar (II Sam. 9:4) and Karnaim (Gen. 14:5). Neither one of these places was very important. Israel had conquered both these cities. They prided themselves on the victories obtained. These exploits made them feel secure.

God will bring up a nation against them. That nation will really test their strength. Again, the prophet does not mention this nation by name, but it is very evident that he means Assyria. Israel may have defeated Lodebar and Karnaim but will be no match for Assyria. This nation will afflict Israel. It will press them. No land will be big enough to hold both Assyria and Israel. When this nation comes against Israel it will afflict the people from the one extreme border to the other. The destruction will be total. Surely, when that day comes it will not be a day of light but a day of thick darkness. Only a people reconciled to their God will be able to look forward to that day.

Questions for Discussion

1. Why does God swear by himself at times? Is this always an indication of something momentous?
2. When does God hate the palaces of a people?
3. Cremation was forbidden in Israel. Are there ever times when that which is otherwise forbidden may be done? Do circumstances determine right and wrong?
4. Did the Israelites mention the name "Jehovah" in later times?
5. Can the arguments which Amos uses in the first six chapters be used against capitalism as a system? Is capitalism Scriptural?
6. Is there a danger that we, as a church, pride ourselves on the accomplishments of former days and become blind to present dangers?

Lesson 17

Amos' Visions of Destruction

Amos 7:1-6

A new section of the book of Amos begins with chapter 7. Before this he has been speaking directly to the people warning them concerning their sins which will make judgment necessary. Now he speaks of several visions which he saw relating to the Israel of his day.

The Lord Jehovah revealed these visions to the prophet. The prophets speak only the word which the Lord has given them to speak; and their visions are only those which the Lord has caused them to see. These visions which Amos saw speak of destruction. The prophet sees the Lord forming locusts. This plague is not due to natural circumstances, but the Lord is forming them! It is a vision which is seen in the spring of the year. The first cutting of hay has been gathered in. This cutting was for the king's stables. This was a good crop and the royal needs are met. The next cutting is for the people. Their livelihood depends on this crop. Now Amos sees this vision! The Lord is forming locusts which will eat every green thing. Amos is alarmed! Does he now wait until the locusts have made an end of all the vegetation? Our translation gives that impression. But then it would be too late. Remember, we are here dealing with a vision. The text might also more properly be translated: "When they would have made an end of eating the grass of the land." Amos does not wait until the destruction is accomplished, but he makes his plea after he has seen the host of locusts.

We often receive the impression that Amos is only a

prophet of indignation. He thunders against the sin of his day. He gives a vivid portrayal of the coming judgments. But Amos is not only a prophet of doom. Though he is an austere man he has a pastoral heart! His heart is full of love for his people. He is not only the stern prophet, he is also a sympathetic priest. Such a man Israel needs — one who portrays sin as it is, and one who can also pray.

As soon as Amos sees the destruction approaching he prays for his people. It is a very brief prayer, but it is the outpouring of a priestly soul. He does not pray: "Oh, Lord, remove the locusts!" No, he sees the reason for the locusts. He prays: "O Lord, forgive!" That is the need. This people deserves destruction. If the locusts are removed, other evils will come. The root of the matter is — sin! The only way this people will be spared is through the forgiving grace of their God. He pleads with the covenant God.

In the previous chapter the prophet spoke of the greatness and strength of Israel. He spoke in irony to the people. Now, when he stands before God, he says the very opposite. How shall Jacob stand? How shall this people ever contend with their God? Jacob is small. Israel has no strength. Israel boasts of its accomplishments. Amos knows better. If God enters into judgment with this people, it will be consumed.

What is the effect of the prophet's prayer? Jehovah repented concerning this. It shall not be, saith Jehovah. Did God change his mind? God doesn't change in his being nor does he change his mind (Malachi 3:6). What does Amos mean by these words? He is not the only Biblical writer who has spoken in this manner. He is simply using human terms in speaking of God so that his ways become understandable to men. Amos' prayer is heard. This evil does not come.

Now Amos receives another vision. Again he sees Jehovah ready to contend with the people by means of fire. The fire of which the prophet speaks is the heat of the sun causing severe drought. This vision is not seen during the spring of the year, but in mid-summer. The heat of the sun can be so scorching that it dries up all vegetation. Amos is now made to see this drought in its most extreme form. It is so great that "the great deep" is devoured. This does not have reference to the seas but to the underground water supply. The water table falls lower and lower. This is the water necessary to life on the ground. As the sun devours this deep it threatens to eat up the land. This will mean famine. The poor, the common people, are the ones who suffer the most when such visitations come. Nothing will grow if this scorching heat comes.

Again the prophet becomes priest. His people are in danger. He is the only one who realizes how great the danger is. The people see no danger threatening their prosperity and security. However, God has revealed it to his prophet. God's judgments are just, but the prophet's love for the people drives him to God's mercy seat. His prayer differs from the previous one. Then he prayed, "O Lord, forgive." Now he cries out, "Cease, I beseech thee." Surely, Amos recognizes this second evil as a judgment on sin as well as the first. We must not conclude that he now loses sight of the need of forgiveness. But the second evil is more intense than the first. It is so terrible that it gives rise to an outcry of the soul, "Cease!" Hold it back! Do not allow this judgment to fall on this people!

Amos pleads on the same basis as formerly. He comes to the covenant God. Jacob will not be able to stand for he is small. If this judgment is carried out, Israel will be consumed.

God had not allowed the previous judgment to come, but will his longsuffering have no end? No, his readiness to forgive is endless. When Amos prays this second time the answer is the same as it was before. This evil is also stayed. Israel must never complain that God had dealt hastily with them. Amos prayed for forgiveness but Israel had not repented. Still God waits. A mere man prays and the God of judgment lays his rod aside. Amos was maligned, but how blessed is the people whose prophet is a priest! Amos here reminds us of the great Highpriest who stood in the breach and reconciled God and man.

Questions for Discussion

1. Why do even God's people often give a natural interpretation of calamities rather than speaking of them as sent by God? Should we see God's hand in all calamities, such as war and sickness?
2. Should a minister be an able intercessor as well as an able preacher? Why doesn't the former receive as much emphasis as the latter?
3. What does Amos teach us when he prays for forgiveness rather than the removal of locusts? Is this type of prayer common with us?
4. What significance is there in the fact that he addresses God as Jehovah covenant God?
5. Amos refers to the weakness of Israel when he prays. Why are we small in our own sight when we are engaged in true prayer? Why does prayer naturally make one humble?

The Vision of the Plumbline

Amos 7:7-9

The third vision which the prophet sees differs from the former ones in various ways. He had seen visions relating to two different seasons. The devastation contained in the first two visions was unmistakable. Amos pleaded with his God that the things which he had seen in vision might not become reality.

Now the picture changes. He now sees the Lord standing by a wall which had been made by a builder with a plumbline in his hand. This picture does not suggest destruction. It looks innocent and harmless.

The wall by which the Lord is standing is the symbol of the whole house of Israel. Israel had been built by the plumbline. The plumbline is the instrument used to determine whether a wall is vertically straight. Israel had been built in such a way that the exacting standard of the plumbline was satisfied. God had given Israel its laws. These laws were exacting. God himself had built the house of Israel. He does not build anything which will not pass exacting inspection. Amos now sees him standing by this wall which had been built correctly. He has a plumbline in his hand. He is going to determine whether that wall, that house, is still true in its vertical lines.

The prophet is asked the question what he sees. He does not speak of the wall; he does not even speak of the Lord himself who is standing by the wall. He mentions only the plumbline. That is the heart of the matter! He realizes that the plumbline will determine the meaning of this vision.

His attention is called to it by the question which is asked. When Jeremiah saw visions he was also asked many times what he saw. This method of teaching centers all the attention on the central part of the vision.

When Amos has responded to the question, God at once gives the interpretation of the vision. Amos is not given an opportunity to intercede for the people. After he had seen the former visions he at once prays for the protection of the people. Now it is different. The former visions needed no interpretation. It was immediately evident that they meant destruction. But destruction is not wrought with a plumbline! Besides, when locusts come or when a great drought threatens, one can still plead that the people are small and that they would not be able to stand. But when a plumbline is used, who can argue with that? Regardless how helpless or small a people may be, it should still be vertically straight! A plumbline is *fair*. It asks no more than that which may be expected. However, it is also very exacting. All deviations from a straight line will be evident at once when a plumbline is used. How can a prophet pray under these circumstances? Surely, he cannot pray, "Lord, do not use the plumbline." God *must*! He is just. He demands that what he has built shall answer to its purpose. He will not allow a wall, of which he is the builder, to be crooked or leaning. That isn't demanding too much!

The Lord tells Amos that he will set the plumbline in the midst of his people. Amos has seen things correctly. The plumbline was the main thing. The wall only completed the picture. The Lord is not going to measure walls, but his people! Amos has been called to speak against the sins of Israel. The sin of this people was great. How great? That is difficult to determine. Everyone could see that Israel was sinning deeply. Virtually everyone will agree that we all sin. But that isn't the question! The question is, how *great* my sin and misery is. That cannot be determined by a casual glance. The human eye is not clear enough to give an answer to that question. To get the right answer a plumbline (the law) has to be used. That plumbline God now sets in the midst of his people. That plumbline doesn't lie. It gives the, exact picture. Prayer does not avail against the law. Amos can only wait.

The prophet doesn't have to wait long. The Lord tells him that he will pass by them no more. Amos had sought forgiveness for his people when he saw the first vision and he obtained it. After the second vision he pleads with his God for mercy toward his people and he obtained it. However, God will not pass by them anymore. He will maintain his right. The law remains standing. Judgment is now fully determined.

The nature of the judgment is now also made clear to the prophet. The high places of Isaac shall be desolate and the sanctuaries of Israel shall be laid waste. These were the places where the people practiced their religion. These were not the places designated by their God, but the places which they themselves had chosen. These places were the pride of Israel. Here they brought their many sacrifices. These places will be destroyed. God strikes at the very heart of Israel's religion. Their false religion lay at the root of the sins they were committing.

Besides accomplishing the destruction of Israel's "holy places," God will also rise against the house of Jeroboam with the sword. Jehu had been appointed king of Israel to rid the land of Ahab's sins. Because he did this, his house became the royal house of Israel for several generations. Jeroboam was the most prosperous of all the kings of Jehu's dynasty. But he was also the one who had forgotten the most important duty imposed on Jehu's house: to maintain righteousness and justice in Israel. God will smite Jeroboam's *house*. His son reigns for six months and this dynasty ends. His servant slays him and reigns in his place.

God's word does not fail.

Amos saw these visions and must tell the people the things which he saw. The evils of locusts and drought were averted, but this judgment will surely come. God is long-suffering, but he is not mocked. Let Israel know that it is getting late. The lights are going out. These visions also belong to the words which Amos *saw* (Amos 1:1).

Questions for Discussion
1. Why must the law of God be preached "so strictly?" (Cf. Q. 115 of the Heidelberg Catechism)
2. In which way had God built Israel originally? Did he also build the New Testament church by the plumbline?
3. When does the time arrive that we are not to intercede? Or does this time never come?
4. How can the individual know *how great* his sin and misery is? Why is this the first thought of the Heidelberg Catechism after the introductory question?
5. How did the royal house add to the sin of Israel?

The Clash of Priest and Prophet

Amos 7:10-17

Suddenly the prophecy of Amos is interrupted. A historical incident is now introduced. To some it seems that this incident is entirely out of place here, but it follows very normally from that which has preceded.

Amos has spoken concerning his visions at Bethel. This is the place of the king's sanctuary and at this place Amaziah is the chief priest. Amos has not only spoken woes on the house of Israel, but he even mentioned the fact that God would rise against the house of Jeroboam with the sword. Amaziah hastens to the king. He tells the king what Amos has said. This is nothing less than treason! The priest does not give an accurate report, but that is explainable. He is upset! The land is not able to bear all the words of Amos, according to Amaziah. This prophet is becoming dangerous!

Now Amaziah speaks to Amos. He has advice for him. Why wait until Jeroboam drives you out of the land? Go, flee into the land of Judah. That was Amos' home. In the eyes of Amaziah he is a seer — one who sees visions — a visionary. Go back to the land of Judah and you can make your living there as a prophet. Amos is prophesying to make a living. He can do that better in Judah. Don't prophesy here because this is the king's sanctuary and a royal house. We don't want to hear your words here. This place of worship is not the place where God's word must be heard! Everything was fine here before you came.

Don't disturb our peace!

This episode gives an indication of the spiritual decay in Israel. The priest is far more concerned about external peace than the truth of God. Silence the prophet! Then they can continue in the way which they desire.

What will Amos do? Will he admit defeat before this churchman? Amaziah has informed him how his words have been received. Amos will not be "successful." He is told to quit and go back home.

Amos is not frightened. He gives the priest a very clear answer. There is good reason why he has preached here in Bethel. True, says Amos, I was not a prophet or the son of a prophet. I was a herdsman and a dresser of sycamore trees. Amos was not a prophet by profession. He did not have to make his living by preaching the word of God. He made his living in a different manner. Therefore, the insinuation that he should go back to Judah and earn his bread there by preaching is based on a false assumption. Nor was it Amos' own idea to come to the northern kingdom to preach. "Jehovah took me… Jehovah said unto me, Go, prophesy unto my people Israel." *That* is the reason why he is here. Jehovah laid hold on him. Jehovah put the words in his mouth. When Jehovah speaks, who can but prophesy? Amos is not a hireling! He has been *sent*!

Had the prophet been a hireling, he would, no doubt, have been frightened and would have fled. But how could a hireling ever speak the words which Amos had spoken? Sufficient hire could not be given a man to speak such words! There is something far more compelling than the desire for bread which has caused Amos to leave his home to warn apostate Israel. The compulsion of Jehovah was upon him. Here is the contrast: sufficient pay could not be given a hireling to do what Amos did; nothing in the world could stop Amos from preaching this word when he had been called by God! That call is necessary for the true prophet. Amaziah has not understood the man Amos. He thought that the prophet was one like himself. Amaziah desired to maintain his position at all costs. Amos is only interested in speaking all the words which Jehovah has given him to speak. The true and the false are here brought face to face.

Religious leaders like Amaziah have brought Israel to its present sad state. Amaziah will not disturb Israel's godlessness. Amos does. But they need an Amos much more than an Amaziah!

Amos is not frightened by the priest nor does he change his approach. The word must be spoken. Even though Jeroboam would rise against him with his soldiers, Amos will be true to his calling. The prophet continues his message. However, he first addresses his words to the chief priest in particular. He does not stand in awe of Amaziah nor of his connections with the royal house. Because this priest has dared to withstand the prophet of God, special woes will fall upon him and his family. You said thus… but Jehovah says this. The words of the priest are contrasted with the words of the living God. They should have been speaking the same words. What will be the result of Amaziah's opposition to the word of God? His wife will be a harlot in the city. The chief priest's wife will be known publicly as a base woman. His family life will be destroyed. His sons and daughters will fall by the sword. That sword which would never come in the estimation of Amaziah would slay his own children. His land, his possessions, will be parceled out to others. He himself will die in an alien land. His house will be utterly ruined. Judgment will be visited more severely on this priest than on virtually any other man. Woe to him who withstands the word of God!

The prophet concludes with the same message which he had given again and again: Israel will surely be led away captive out of his land. Amaziah's interruption has not changed things in the least. The people must realize that nothing can stop the word of God. This word will be spoken and this word will be fulfilled. They must not seek to silence the prophet; they must repent!

Too often there has been the attempt to silence the prophets of God. This has always been disastrous for those who attempted it. God causes his word to go forth and he will also protect those whom he calls to proclaim that word.

Questions for Discussion

1. Why would Amaziah wish Amos to leave?
2. Is there danger that we will have places or situations where we do not wish to hear the word of God?
3. Should anyone enter the ministry who can avoid it?
4. May ministers ever consider their work as their livelihood? Do church members ever consider the minister's work to be such?
5. What made Amos so fearless?

A Basket of Summer Fruit

Amos 8:1-3

Three separate visions had been shown the prophet concerning Israel's future. Then there was an interruption as the chief priest of Bethel sought to persuade the prophet to leave. After Amos had answered Amaziah the visions continue.

The vision which he now sees differs from the former in several ways. The first two visions revealed unmistakable judgment. As a result, Amos pleads with his God that his people may be spared. The third vision was more innocent in appearance. In that vision he saw a man standing by a wall with a plumbline in his hand. This is not an instrument of destruction, but it is nevertheless disturbing. The plumbline will be used to see whether or not the wall is straight. Now the prophet sees something entirely different. He sees a basket of summer fruit. The first vision spoke of spring, the second of mid-summer, and the fourth of the fall of the year. There is nothing disturbing in a vision of summer fruit. It is, in fact, evidence that the earth has brought forth abundantly. It is decidedly attractive.

All these visions give a picture of the house of Israel. Amos relates to the people at Bethel the things he has seen. Has the warning of Amaziah had this effect on the prophet that he now gives an ideal picture of Israel? Has he become afraid? Does he, in effect, now say: disregard the picture given in the former visions, because Israel is like a beautiful basket of ripe fruit? We know the prophet better than that! He will speak that which he "sees." Even though the message may be very unpopular, Amos will speak all the words which Jehovah gives him to speak. His answer to Amaziah gave clear proof that he was not afraid of the criticism of this high "churchman."

Amos now sees a very innocent looking vision — a basket of summer fruit. This looks both innocent and prosperous. That is the picture of Israel. Externally everything did look good. Israel's prosperity has been noted before. When one looks at Israel he will notice nothing amiss. This vision, this illustration, pictures Israel exactly. When God chooses illustrations they are perfect!

The heart of the matter lies in the ripeness of the fruit which Amos sees. That fruit is not growing anymore; it is ripe and it is ready to be eaten. In the Hebrew there is a play on words. As this fruit is ripe, so also the people of Israel is ripe. Here they are spoken of as being ripe for destruction. The emphasis does not fall on the sin committed, but on the punishment for the sin. The prophet is given a vision of ripe fruit; so Israel is ripe for destruction. God has given his judgment. As a result, he will not pass by them anymore. It has been decided. There is no way by which Israel will escape punishment.

After the first two visions the prophet could plead for his people. After the third vision this is not permitted. He measured Israel with the plumbline. What will the verdict be? That verdict we now hear in this vision. These four visions, therefore, do not come with the same message. There is progress. This fourth vision, which appeared to be the most harmless and innocent, is in fact the most fearful. The punishment will come because Israel is ripe for it. The prophet must agree. No plea can be offered for a people that continues in sin despite all warnings.

Now that punishment will surely come on this people, in that way at times. We have only to think of the third commandment as an example. However, it is clearly revealed to Amos what the punishment will be.

The punishment will fit the crime. The people will be punished according to their doings. No one will be able to say that the punishment was too severe nor that it did not suffice. God is just. He maintains his justice regardless of circumstances. His grace does not overthrow his justice, neither does his justice make grace impossible. He brings the two into a beautiful harmony.

The songs in the temple at Bethel have been many. The people "enjoyed" their religion. They were very careful that all the forms of religion were observed. If the forms were observed then surely everything would be all right! God would look on them in favor. Besides this, they were so "grateful" to their God for all the blessings he had sent that they responded with music and offerings. But their fundamental error was made in the realm of their religion. It was offensive to the God whom they supposedly worshiped. This is the area in which the judgment will fall first. The songs of the temple will be changed into wailings. The people have looked longingly for "the day of Jehovah" (5:18). That is the day when their songs will be turned into wailings. This is not only Amos' idea; this is the word which Jehovah himself has spoken. Silencing the prophets does not help. They only relate what God has spoken.

The prophet even tells us what the content of their wailing will be. It will be: "dead bodies... everywhere." The prophet becomes very abrupt in his style. This is in keeping with the nature of the evil which. will come. Songs become wailings. Nor does he speak of an indefinite "they," but rather, "he shall cast them forth." These are the dead bodies of those who have perhaps been slain by the pestilence.

At the conclusion of verse three he commands, "Silence!" When these calamities come, it will behoove them to be silent. This is not the kind of silence which roots in a superstitious fear of naming the name of Jehovah (6:10), but rather a reverent silence as Jehovah smites.

How different the "day of Jehovah" will be from what they had expected! Instead of singing songs, they will be dumb with mourning. This is the result of their failure to repent. Form-religion ruined them. It blinded their eyes to danger and finally slew them.

Questions for Discussion

1. Should the message of the word ever be "toned down" if there are dangers that the word might offend? In how far can we subscribe to a "psychological approach?"
2. Are illustrations always helpful or can they also be harmful? Did the parables of Jesus clarify or obscure?
3. How does God harmonize justice and grace? Can we still speak of forgiveness when the debt is paid by Christ?
4. Why is "form religion" so dangerous? Is there danger of this evil today?

Lesson 21

The Thoughts of Worshippers

Amos 8:4-10

In these Verses Amos pictures the Israelites of his day
as they observe their religious feasts and the sabbath.
As has been noted before, the people are very religious.
The sabbath was the important day in their religious life.
That day was not neglected. They closed their places of
business and went to their places of worship. This was done
in obedience to the law of God... no work, no business
on the sabbath. They respected this law and would not
have thought of violating it by conducting their business on
the day which God had chosen for himself. Outwardly the
law was kept.

The prophet, however, does not only look upon the
outward observance of the holy days, but he is also
interested in their thoughts as they are engaged in worship.
Have they also closed their minds to the affairs of the world
of business as they closed their shop doors the previous
evening? Is the mind now centered on the word of the living
God? Is this the day on which they will be strengthened
spiritually to cope with the world about them on the
following days?

Their thoughts do not wander while they are worshipping;
they are fixed on the world of business! While they sing lustily:

My soul longeth, yea, even fainteth for the courts of

Jehovah; My heart and flesh cry out unto the living God —
They think: When will this new moon or this sabbath be past!
This day must be kept, but how irksome, how tedious!

There is no profit in this day. They can scarcely wait for the end of the day of rest.

While they are worshipping their thoughts are with their business. While they are worshipping they are devising corrupt business practices! Here in God's house they are making plans to make more money. They desire to get busy again to display and to sell their grain. By their evil business tactics they swallow up the needy and cause the poor of the land to fail. How do they do this? The prophet makes it very clear. They use a small measure (ephah) to measure out the grain to the buyer. He is not getting full measure. Besides this, they use a heavy shekel. The buyers came with their silver, but this silver was weighed against a shekel which was too heavy. To put it in today's terms, they used a bushel which was too small, so that the buyer did not get a bushel; and they obtained more money than a bushel was worth. Even the product which they sell is inferior. They sell the refuse of the wheat. This is the wheat of inferior quality. Even this they sell at an exorbitant price.

If this practice continues for any length of time, the poor and needy are swallowed up. This practice brings its victims to poverty. Finally, the poor will have insufficient money to buy the necessities of life. He will then have to sell himself. Thus the poor are bought for silver. For the price of a pair of shoes the needy will have to sell themselves. Where corrupt economic practices are found the whole social structure will ultimately be ruined.

All these things they contemplate while they are engaged in worship! The sabbath is no delight to them, but rather a burden. Externally they are religious — religious customs and traditions are honored — but inwardly they rebel. No, they would not think of keeping their business places open for business on the sabbath, but all their thoughts and desires are behind the closed doors of their shops. This is formalism at its worst!

What is the divine reaction to all this? Jehovah swears by the excellency of Jacob, therefore by himself, that he will never forget any of their works. When he forgives, he forgets; but his memory can also be very long. He will not overlook this sin. It is grievous.

Will not the land tremble and its inhabitants mourn for this grievous sin? Isn't this sinning beyond all limits? Has anyone ever heard anything like it? Now the prophet reveals the nature of the punishment for this sin. The evil that is coming will be like an earthquake. The ground underfoot will rise and sink like the waters of the Nile river when it overflows its banks and becomes a tremendously large body of water. Like the waves on such a body of water, so shall the ground be on which they stand.

Not only will the earth shake under their feet, but the heavens above will also show their displeasure. The sun will go down at noon. The earth will become dark during the clear day. This will be totally unnatural. Men will quake with fear. The ground beneath gives no stability and the skies above are dark when they should be light.

Their feasts will be changed into mourning. These feasts, which they formerly considered to be boring, will be turned into times of mourning. Their songs will be changed into lamentations. They sang these songs with their lips but not with their hearts. These same songs will become bitter lamentations. In keeping with the time of mourning and the singing of lamentations, they will be dressed in sack-cloth. They will shave their heads as an expression, of their grief. Their worship had been unreal. Their grief will be real. It will be like the mourning for an only son. There is no greater grief. Where there is mourning for an only son the believer may even then find comfort. Not so in Israel. The end is as a bitter day. There is no comfort. The mourning continues without end.

The people had often longed for the day of Jehovah

to come. This is what that day will be like for them (vss. 9, 10). Why? Because they had sinned more grievously than the heathen. The heathen doesn't worship the true God. Israel worshiped the true God falsely. Its worship is exacting because they worship him who sees the heart. Men can sin deeply while worshipping. "Keep thy foot when thou goest to the house of God." It is so easy "to bring the sacrifice of fools." This Israel did. Its punishment would be severe.

Questions for Discussion
1. Is it humanly possible to keep our thoughts from wandering during an entire service of worship? If not, is this sin?
2. How and when should we prepare for worship?
3. How can the sabbath be a delight to us?
4. The Apostle James teaches us that the love of money is a root of all evil. How is this revealed in this passage?
5. Does the fact that Jehovah will never forget their works mean that forgiveness has become impossible?
6. Did all these evils spoken of actually come upon Israel?

Lesson 22

A Unique Famine

Amos 8:11-14

Although the land of Palestine had often been described as the land flowing with milk and honey, the experience of famine was not foreign to its people. At different times the patriarchs had to leave the land because famine was raging. Famine had been sent at times as a punishment for sin. In chapter four Amos spoke of famine which God had sent to turn the people to himself again. Israel had so hardened its heart that they did not turn to God.

In the previous verses Amos had described the "day of Jehovah" as it would come upon this people. It will be a day of comfortless mourning. In the verses 11-14 he gives a further characterization of that "day," or that period of time.

God will send a famine on this land which will be more severe than any famine before. It will not be of the same nature as other famines. The common conception of a famine is this that there is a scarcity of food and water. That is a terrible calamity. It is the time when one must forego the necessities of life, when one sees his children starving. But this famine will be different. It will consist of a scarcity of the Word of God! In former days when they had the Word, they ignored it. Amaziah told Amos to keep still (see 7:10-13). The people had no desire to hear it. That is the reason for the coming of the famine which the Lord will send.

Seeing that the people have ignored the Word in the past, will it be a real hardship for them to do without it? Haven't they even desired this famine? It is true that they

85

lived without the Word formerly. That Word is often likened
to food but in the past they lived without it by choice.
Are these people going to feel the effect of such a famine?

One would suppose that such a famine would be the least
concern to this people. However, Amos teaches us
differently. They will wander from sea to sea, from the
north to the east; they will run to and fro seeking the Word
of God. Have they changed their attitude toward that
Word? Their desire for it is pictured as being as strong as
the hunger for bread and a thirst for water. They become
frantic in their search. Do they now answer to the ideal of
Jesus as "hungering and thirsting for righteousness?"
Are they now longing as newborn babes for the spiritual
milk? It seems so. They certainly realize that there is a
famine. They miss the Word. Those who sincerely seek it
will find it but of these it is said that they will not find it.

These people are not seeking that Word with a sincere
desire to live according to it and to find their life in it.
They are like Saul, the first king of Israel. He had spurned
the Word of God. Yet, he discovered that he could not live
without it. He became frantic in his search for a revelation.
It finally led him to the witch at Endor. Nevertheless, he did
not find the Word of God. Here is the heart of the whole
matter. When the Word was present they ignored it or
rebelled against it; now that it is taken away, they find they
cannot live without it. Their mourning knows no end.
Oh, that God might say something! What a pitiable state!
This is the famine he will send, and this unique famine is
much worse than any other.

There is a finality about this famine. The people of Israel
will not find the Word of God. He does not allow them to
find it. Though they criss-cross the land, they are
unsuccessful. Grace does have an end. God will not always
be mocked! The former attitude of the people makes it
impossible for them to find the Word now.

In their calamities they realize that they *must* have the Word of God. There is absolutely nothing that can take its place. Satan makes many attacks on the Word of God but he has no substitute for it. This leaves the unbeliever comfortless at the time of his greatest need. How this lack affects the people is vividly described. The fair virgins and the young men will faint for thirst. The fairest and strongest will be consumed. What will then be the condition of the others? As the common famine is no respecter of persons, so this famine also will consume all the people. As in a common famine people faint for thirst, so great will be the thirst for God's Word. Formerly they didn't want it; now they can't do without it. This thirst will not be satisfied.

Amos uses some strange terminology in this section. He does not say that the people will wander from the north to the south, but from the north to the east. It is difficult to state whether this is only a shortened form of north to south and east to west, or whether it is based on the geography of Palestine. He also speaks of the people swearing "by the sin of Samaria." Here the prophet definitely refers to the religion established in the northern kingdom. The people may call it what they will, to the prophet it is the "sin" of Samaria.

In the previous verse Amos spoke of the effect of the famine on the young men and virgins of Samaria. What will be the effect on the rest of the people? He mentions the rest of the people in connection with their religion. There are those who swear by the sin of Samaria. They also swear by the god of Dan. Bethel's god is the god of Samaria. Dan's god does not have the same importance. At both places idolatry is practiced. Some of the people even make pilgrimages to Beersheba. To do this they must travel through the whole land of Judah. This pilgrimage is considered meritorious. They swear by it.

Those who have made themselves guilty of practicing this

false religion will experience the effects of the famine of the Word. They will fall and never rise again. Although the land brings forth by handfuls, they will starve because the Word of God is wanting.

Questions for Discussion

1. Why did Israel seek the Word if they did not have faith to accept it?
2. Is there danger that America will be punished by a famine of the Word?
3. Can the unbeliever live without the Word of God? What effect does the absence of the Word have on the culture of a people?
4. Can men believe "if they want to?"
5. How does a famine of the Word come about? If the government would have all Bibles burned, would that produce a famine of the Word? Is it possible to have a famine of the Word with a Bible in every home?

Inescapable Punishment

Amos 9:1-10

Will this prophet never cease to speak of the evil which will
befall Israel? Has he not made it very clear in the past?
Will the day never dawn?

Yes, the dawn will come but the darkness becomes even
more intense before the coming of the dawn. Amos has seen
four visions concerning the future of Israel. The fifth vision
is now recorded. This one is more awful than the previous
ones. He sees God standing beside the altar. The prophet
does not mention where this altar was and it matters little.
He does not see God as the covenant God but as the
majestic One. When he sees him he speaks. Again, the
prophet does not tell us whom God is addressing. All the
emphasis falls on the words which he speaks. Terrible
words! He says: "Smite the capitals that the thresholds may
shake; and break them in pieces on the head of all of
them." The picture is this: The people come in large
numbers to their place of worship. They are not all able to
get in. God now commands someone to smite that part of
the building which supports the roof and ties the wall
together. So the whole building collapses on the heads of
those who worship. Those who were not able to find room
inside will not escape. He will slay them with the sword.
None will flee away or escape. They are smitten while they
worship. The horns of the altar no longer offer asylum.
This is the last vision and, surely, no more are needed!

To make it clear that the punishment will be inescapable,
the Lord now goes into detail. He will show the people that

there is simply no way out. These words remind one of Psalm 139. Even though these people could dig down into the realm of the dead, they would be brought up from thence by the hand of God to face punishment. If, on the other hand, they would be able to climb up into heaven, it would offer them no refuge. God's hand would bring them down. If they would hide in the woods and caves of Carmel, he would find them. Should there be those who would leap from Carmel into the depths of the Mediterranean Sea, he would command a sea monster to slay them. Not even captivity will safeguard them against the avenging hand of God. His omnipresence is a source of the greatest comfort to the believer, but it is a source of terror to the wicked. When his eye is upon the people for evil, there is no escape.

How will anyone ever strive with God? Notice who he is. He touches the land and it melts. This causes all the inhabitants to mourn. He sends great upheavals (8:8) so that the earth appears as the waves on a broad body of water. This is the God who is enthroned in the heavens. He has made all things. He takes the waters of the seas and pours them out on the dry land as at the time of the flood. Who would ever be able to oppose such a one successfully? How can man be so foolish as to strive with this God? His name is Jehovah, God of the covenant, but it is a name to be feared by those who oppose him. This God-concept is clear throughout the book of Amos. The prophet heard this God speak and he had to prophesy.

This people (Israel) is like the Ethiopians in the sight of God. What? Does Israel not have a special place in his affection? Can it now be said that there is no difference between this covenant people and such an inconsequential people as the Ethiopians? At the time when Amos lived these people had not yet attained to an important position among the nations. But Israel is no better, according to the prophet. Does then the past mean nothing? Had not God led them out of the bondage of Egypt into this land where they now dwell? Yes, but they are not the only people who can speak of an exodus in their history. God had led the Philistines out of Caphtor (Crete?) and the Syrians out of Kir. Surely, the mere fact of their exodus will not give them a privileged position among the nations. Past history is no guarantee of present salvation!

Israel is a sinful kingdom. This has been Amos' contention throughout and he has proved it in many ways. God's eyes are on this sinful kingdom. He is aware of all that takes place. Despite their glorious past, they are a sinful nation. It will be destroyed from off the face of the earth. There is no escape for the sinner. However, the first streaks of dawn now appear. It is not yet light, but there is a promise of better things to come. The sinful kingdom will be destroyed, but God will not utterly exterminate the house of Jacob! Sin will be purged. There is no room for the sin of Israel in the presence of their God. Yet, a remnant will be spared.

How will this be accomplished? There is much difference of opinion regarding the translation and interpretation of verse 9. God here speaks of sifting his people. They will be sifted among the nations. Some think of a small sieve which will not allow the grain to fall through. Others think of a larger sieve which permits the grain to fall through but screens out the stones, of which none will then fall on the ground. The meaning is clear. There is much in Israel which will prove to be refuse when the sieve is used. However, there is some good grain. This will be saved. The good will not perish with the evil. There are still those who are the objects of God's grace. He will not utterly destroy Jacob.

Let no one think that now the punishment will be lightened for all. God has declared judgment on the evil doers. This declaration stands. All the sinners among Israel will die by the sword. Who are they? They are the ones who have turned a deaf ear to the words of the prophet. These are the ones who said, "It can't happen here." For these there is no escape. These are unrepentant. These have simply ignored the Word of God. They felt that God owed them a debt of gratitude for their "piety." For such there is no hope.

Questions for Discussion

1. Is there any similarity between the visions of Amos and some of the parables of Jesus?
2. Why does the most severe punishment fall on those who are in the temple?
3. Are *all* the attributes of God distressing to the unbeliever?
4. How much does one's conception of God determine his religion? Would you say that the question: Who is God? is fundamental?
5. The Ethiopians were black. Does the reference to them in this passage have anything to teach us in regard to the race issue?
6. Did the northern kingdom become "the ten lost tribes?" Were any people in Israel in later years able to trace their ancestry to these tribes?

Lesson 24

The Glorious Future

Amos 9:11-15

Although Amos has denounced Israel for its sins and the crashing of the judgment is heard throughout this book, he concludes his prophecy on a different note. The prophet unmasks sin but also speaks comfort. He does not only use the first key of the kingdom to close the door to the wicked and unbelieving; he also opens the door to those who repent and believe.

The day of Jehovah for which Israel has longed will be utter darkness. But a better day will dawn. Amos now describes the state of David's house. That house of David had been glorious. Its glory was found in the fact that Jehovah himself had built that house (II Sam. 7). Due to the sins committed through the years that house is now found to be in disrepair. It is now "the tabernacle of David that is fallen." The Revised Standard Version translates it: "booth of David." Its glory has departed. It has been ruined from *within*. The people may object to this characterization, but the prophet sees things as they are.

That tabernacle, that booth, that is fallen will be raised up. Destruction is not the last word. God will cement the cracks, the breaches, which have appeared in its walls. He will raise up the ruins, that which was broken off. It will be rebuilt and be as it was in former days. God's work will not fail. Even though the picture drawn by the prophet was very dark, the light now breaks through.

Amos speaks of the fulfillment of this prophecy in true Old Testament terminology. His language can be understood

93

by the people of his day. He speaks of this future of Israel in natural, material terms. So the Old Testament speaks constantly. The promises to Abraham are also couched in terms of material possession. James, the brother of our Lord, quotes this prophecy in Acts 15. He shows us that this prophecy is of great significance for the New Testament church.

Not only will this tabernacle of David be rebuilt, but the meaning of this rebuilding is also made clear. Israel will again possess the remnant of Edom. It will possess all the nations which are called by the name of Jehovah. What does the prophet mean by this? The nations called by the name of Jehovah, or rather, the nations upon whom the name of Jehovah has been called, are those nations which were subjected by Israel in former days. The name of the God of this conquering nation, Israel, was called the name of the God of the defeated nation, as an indication of his victory. Edom alone is mentioned by name. Edom was more closely related to Israel than any of the other nations. It was a special grief to Israel when Edom cast off its yoke of subjection to Israel. In the future Israel will again be the prominent nation as in the past.

As the prophet describes the restoration of Israel in the future, we are reminded of the words found in Lev. 26:5 and Joel 3:18. In these passages the prosperity of those who fear God is pictured. The plowman will overtake the reaper, according to Amos. The harvest will be so great that the people will still be busy reaping the grain of the former year when the time to plow is again upon them. While they are still sowing the grapes will be ripe. There is no period of inactivity, no period without profit. The mountains will drop sweet wine and all the hills will melt. Every piece of land will bring forth in abundance. It will be a time of great prosperity. What a change! The former days were those in which nothing succeeded. Where the favor of Jehovah is, there is peace, love, and prosperity.

These blessings will not come *instead* of the evils spoken of formerly. Amos does not contradict himself. Israel will surely go into captivity but it will return from this captivity. Jehovah will bring back the captivity of his people. Why will his people return? Van Gelderen, a great Old Testament scholar, translates the first part of verse 14 so as to mean that God will remove the sins of Israel, his people. That is the heart of the matter. Only forgiveness can restore the people of God to the land which had been promised them. Did the ten northern tribes ever return from captivity? History teaches us that they did not return as a people. However, although Amos speaks first. of all to the northern kingdom, his prophecy is not exclusively directed to this kingdom. Besides, when James quotes this prophecy he applies it to the Gentiles. Is it not true that Israel "returns" as the Gentiles are brought into the church of Jesus Christ (see Acts 15:13-18)?

The cities which had been wasted at the time of Israel's defeat will be rebuilt and Israel will inhabit these cities. Not only will they plant vineyards, but they will drink the wine they produce. Gardens will be planted and the fruit will be enjoyed. They will, therefore, *remain* in the land. It will not be labor for naught. The fruit of their labors will be enjoyed.

God himself will plant them on the land which he had promised to their fathers. His promises stand. He does not forget the covenant made with the fathers. When he has brought the people back, they will stay there. They will not be plucked up again. Jehovah, their God, has said it and he will perform it!

How beautiful is this book of Amos! God sends him to condemn the sins of this people. He cannot keep silence. Nevertheless, his heart grieves as he sees the judgments approaching. He may now conclude his book with a beautiful picture of the future restoration of Israel.

When Amos denounces the sins of Israel he speaks in unmistakable language. Truly, he shows the people how great their sins and miseries are. His pastoral heart can also bleed for this people. Stirring is his description of the blessed future! Such preachers the church needs.

Sin has been portrayed as it really is. But... there is forgiveness. How Amos would have rejoiced to see the day of Jesus Christ!

Questions for Discussion

1. Why didn't the people of Amos' day consider the nation to be "the tabernacle of David?"
2. How was the house of David ruined from within? How can the church be ruined from within?
3. Why does the Old Testament speak of future glory in natural or material terms?
4. In which ways was Amos the true preacher of the Word? Is such preaching very popular?
5. Is the preaching on sin sufficiently specific today?

Notes

Notes

Notes